Contents

Preface

This booklet consists of a selection of articles that appeared in the *Militant* newspaper in 1997—the year of the 30th anniversary of the death in combat in Bolivia of Ernesto Che Guevara and his comrades. They deal with the Cuban revolution, its impact on world politics, and the communist course charted by its leadership.

Guevara, who was Argentine by birth, joined the July 26 Movement, the Cuban revolutionary movement headed by Fidel Castro, in 1955. Che, as he was popularly known, became one of the central leaders of the insurrectionary struggle that brought down the U.S.-backed Batista dictatorship in 1959. As Cuba's workers and peasants carried out a sweeping land reform and implemented other popular measures that impinged on the prerogatives of U.S. and Cuban property owners, aggression from Washington escalated. The leadership in Cuba responded by deepening the revolutionary struggle, and the first socialist revolution in the Americas was born.

Guevara, side-by-side with Fidel Castro, was among the most capable and far-sighted leaders of that turning point in the history of the 20th century. Between 1959 and 1965 he shouldered many different and important responsibilities in the new revolutionary government, including president of the National Bank, Minister of Industry, military commander, and representative of the government at many international forums and events.

In 1965 Guevara resigned his government, party, and military leadership responsibilities in Cuba and left the country, volunteering his efforts to advance revolutionary struggles elsewhere. He first led a group of Cuban internationalist volunteers who aided the anti-imperialist struggle in the newly independent Congo.

In 1966–67, he led a nucleus of revolutionaries from Bolivia, Cuba, and Peru who fought to overthrow the military dictatorship in Bolivia. In the process of that struggle, they sought to forge a Latin America–wide movement of workers and peasants that could lead the battle for land reform and against U.S. imperialist domination of the continent and advance the struggle for socialism world-wide. They were also seeking to aid the revolutionary struggle of the people of Vietnam, then waging a historic, and eventually successful, battle against U.S. imperialist aggression. Guevara was wounded and captured on Oct. 8, 1967. He was shot the next day by the Bolivian military, after consultation with Washington.

Those interested in knowing more about the revolutionary campaign in Bolivia can turn to the pages of Guevara's *Bolivian Diary* and *Pombo: A Man of Che's 'Guerrilla,'* by Cuban brigadier general Harry Villegas, who fought with Che in Bolivia. Along with other books of Guevara's speeches and writings, such as *Episodes of the Cuban Revolutionary War, Che Guevara Speaks, Socialism and Man in Cuba, To Speak the Truth: Why Washington's 'Cold War' Against Cuba Doesn't End,* and other titles published by Pathfinder Press, these works provide an irreplaceable communist perpsective on the Cuban revolution and its place in history. (See ads at the end of this booklet).

Among the activities in Cuba that commemorated the 30th anniversary of Che's combat in Bolivia were numerous political events organized by the Communist Party of Cuba and other mass organizations—including the 12,000-strong World Festival of Youth and Students, and the International Workers' Meeting to Confront Neoliberalism and Globalization, sponsored by the Central Organization of Cuban Workers (CTC). *Part I* of this compilation includes reports on two of the most important of these gatherings, each of which helped advance the Cuban revolution and the world struggle for socialism.

The first article reports on the international workshop "Socialism as the 21st Century Approaches," which took place Oct. 21–23, 1997. The second article is the *Militant*'s account of the Fifth Congress of the Communist Party of Cuba, which opened two weeks earlier on the anniversary of Guevara's death. This section also contains the greetings from the National Committee of the Socialist Workers Party to that congress. Part I concludes with a review of *Secrets of the Generals*, published in Cuba in early 1997. This is a book in which 41 generals of Cuba's Revolutionary Armed Forces (FAR) talk about how and why they joined the revolutionary struggle in Cuba and tell of their political and combat experiences in many parts of the world over a number of years as soldiers in the international proletarian army Che and Fidel helped lead.

As part of the commemoration of this 30th anniversary year in Cuba, dozens of articles, speeches, and interviews by those who knew and worked with Che were published in a broad range of publications. Many of Guevara's collaborators as well as family members spoke at conferences and other meetings, bringing Che to life for a new generation and explaining the importance of his communist political legacy today. Valuable firsthand accounts by revolutionists, containing details and observations that enrich our knowledge and understanding of the dynamics of the class struggle in the early years of the revolution, were written down and published for the first time. They are part of the broader discussion taking place in Cuba on how to advance the revolution today.

The *Militant* reprinted a selection of these contributions as a weekly feature, under the rubric "Che Guevara and the Cuban Revolution." The entire twelve-part series is reproduced in *Part II* of this compilation, including the final contribution, an article by revolutionary leader and former President of Algeria Ahmed Ben Bella on "Che Guevara, Cuba, and the Algerian revolution," which appeared in *Militant* Vol. 62, no. 4, dated Feb. 2, 1998.

The *Militant* extends special thanks to its longtime comrade Robin Maisel who suggested that these articles be collected. More important than the idea (raised by other readers as well), he volunteered his time and organizing experience to collaborate with socialist workers, Young Socialists and other *Militant* supporters in California to raise the funds necessary to make the idea a reality, and the enthusiastic distribution of this collection an assured success.

Mary-Alice Waters
JANUARY 19, 1998

PART I

COMMUNIST PARTY OF CUBA HOSTS FORUM ON ROAD TO WORLD STRUGGLE FOR SOCIALISM

by Jack Barnes and Mary-Alice Waters

HAVANA—"In the present international conditions, we reaffirm that socialism is a necessity," said Cuban leader José Ramón Balaguer. "Not only is it the logical result of the development of productive forces on an international scale, it is also the only alternative to guarantee the survival of humanity."

Balaguer, a member of the Political Bureau of the Central Committee of the Communist Party of Cuba, gave the keynote address to the October 21–23 international workshop here on "Socialism as the 21st Century Approaches."

On a world scale, Balaguer emphasized, the growing global contradictions of capitalism—economic, social, and political—and internal class conflicts do not point toward increased stability and accommodation to the needs of working people. Rather, these are more and more weighty factors "stimulating the struggle for a new social order," he noted.

"The contradiction between capital and labor is increasingly internationalized," he continued, "making imperative an in-depth study of socialism, beyond national borders and contradictions, and confirming the relevance of that slogan of classic Marxism: 'Workers of all countries, unite!'—which,

MILITANT/MARY-ALICE WATERS

Socialism is the "only alternative to guarantee the survival of humanity," José Ramón Balaguer told participants in international workshop on Socialism as the 21st Century Approaches.

Reprinted from *Militant* vol. 61, no. 41, Dec. 24, 1997.

far from being outdated, could be extended, drawing in other social sectors and movements that are also subjected to the barbarity of capital."

Emphasizing that socialism is not simply a matter of economics, Balaguer underlined the critical need for the revolutionary workers movement to take the moral high ground falsely claimed by the ideologues transfixed by the aura of the exploiters and oppressors. He stressed the obligation "to show not only the possibility and viability of socialism, but also its desirability."

"For us, socialism is the only possible and valid option for placing social relations on a moral footing," he noted. "We cannot relax our efforts to demonstrate on a theoretical and practical level its superiority in fact in developing the highest of human values: justice, equality, fairness, freedom, democracy, respect for human rights, national sovereignty, solidarity."

The conference, attended by more than 200 participants from around the world, was one of a series of political gatherings that have taken place in Cuba over the last months. These began with the 12,000-strong International Festival of Youth and Students last July. It continued through the August international meeting of trade unionists sponsored by the Central Organization of Cuban Workers under the rubric of Workers Against Neoliberalism and Globalization; conferences on the legacy and relevance of the work of Argentine-Cuban leader Ernesto Che Guevara; the fifth congress of the Communist Party of Cuba; and the solemn ceremonies in mid-October during which Cubans and others around the world paid tribute to Guevara and the revolutionists who fought and died with him 30 years ago in Bolivia, as their remains were transferred to and interred in the city of Santa Clara.

Above all, the character and content of these conferences and other events began to confront the political confusion that has marked the leadership of broad popular movements in recent years, in Latin America and throughout the world. They reflected the broadening social and economic struggles that offer real possibilities of moving forward.

Overawed by the seeming wealth and power of the world capitalist order, and disoriented by incomprehension of the implosion of the bureaucratic regimes of Eastern Europe and the Soviet Union, the crisis of leadership within the workers movement has manifested itself, country after country, in the tendency toward worship of the existing fact. Radical rhetoric and accommodation, not revolutionary resistance and organization, has prevailed—even as the crisis of the imperialist system has deepened and the decline of popular struggles has bottomed out.

The initiatives taken by the leadership of the Communist Party of Cuba, however, have pointed in the opposite direction from this centrist capitulation, advancing efforts to find concrete points of agreement in common struggle out of which new alliances can be forged.

The leadership time and material resources that have gone into these important events would have been impossible in Cuba even a year ago. It is only now, as the worst years of the economic and political crisis precipitated by the collapse of the regimes and parties in Eastern Europe and the Soviet Union begin to recede, that such an effort can be sustained. The relief from the extreme tensions of the last years, when all energies were concentrated on the battle for beans and potatoes, is palpable to returning visitors.

The year of the 30th anniversary of the death in combat of Ernesto Che Guevara and his comrades has become the occasion to celebrate, in a dignified and deeply determined manner, the fact that a corner has been turned, the worst of what is known in Cuba as the special period has been faced and conquered. Even more, it has become the moment for the communist vanguard of Cuba's workers and farmers to solemnly reaffirm the revolutionary socialist and internationalist course that the entire Cuban leadership, Guevara included, have fought to defend for more than 40 years, and to draw revolutionists worldwide into the international leadership responsibilities they shoulder in a world where new battles are on the horizon.

World gathering

Some 97 parties and other political organizations, as well as a number of academic or independently sponsored think tanks, responded to the invitation of the Communist Party of Cuba and its cadre school, the Ñico López School of Higher Learning, to take part in the international workshop. Its purpose was "to discuss socialism as a real alternative to the existing capitalist society."

The largest participation came from South America, with representatives of parties from every country where Spanish or Portuguese is the main language. From most countries, there were delegates from several political organizations with whom the Communist Party of Cuba maintains fraternal relations. Central America and the non-Spanish-speaking Caribbean were under-represented by contrast, and there were no delegates from parties in Guatemala, Honduras, or Nicaragua.

From the United States, delegates represented the Socialist Workers Party, Workers World, Committees of Correspondence, All African Peoples' Revolutionary Party, Socialist Action, and Freedom Socialist Party. From Canada, the Communist League, the Communist Party of Canada (Marxist-Leninist), and Socialist Action took part.

From Africa, delegates came from Zimbabwe, Angola, and Ghana. Representatives of governing parties in China, Vietnam, Laos, and the Democratic People's Republic of Korea took part, as did political organizations from South Korea, India, Turkey, and Palestine. There were no delegates present from Australia, New Zealand, Indonesia, or Japan.

The Communist parties of many countries of Europe, including Russia and the Czech Republic, were represented by one, and in a few cases more, delegates, but only a sprinkling of other political organizations in Europe were present. From the United Kingdom, the Communist League and Revolutionary Communist Group sent delegates. Denmark was the only Nordic country represented.

Balaguer's opening remarks on behalf of the Communist Party of Cuba introduced the main themes of discussion and offered a sharp political focus for the commission sessions that followed. The topics for the three different commissions were broadly defined as "Realities of Contemporary Socialism," "The Relevance of Marxist and Leninist Thought and Contemporary Marxists," and "Imperialism at the End of the Millennium."

For the most part, divergent political views held by the wide array of parties and individuals in attendance were addressed in an indirect exchange through 15-minute summary presentations made by spokespeople for each of the organizations. Over the course of the three days, however, a number of the questions introduced by Balaguer in his keynote became the center of more direct exchanges in some of the commissions.

Globalization and nation-states

After calling attention to the fact that many phenomena are bundled together under the "fashionable" banner of "globalization," Balaguer noted that from the beginning of the modern workers movement Marxism has "alerted us to the fact that the growth of the network of international economic relations is an objective process of capitalism. The international character of capital—one of its defining features—made it possible for capitalist rule to take on, as one of its ingredients, the establishment of a world system, the first, to be exact, in the history of humanity. That same international character, backed today by colossal advances in science and technology, has resulted in a very high degree of internationalization of capital."

But globalization does not imply the diminished importance of the state, he emphasized. "In the name of some future 'global village,' an image that brings to mind turn-of-the-century arguments regarding 'superimperialism,' we are told of a new world economy—where an atmosphere of permanent harmony will be possible, both between countries and within them—resulting from the end of the Cold War. Moreover, it is assumed that, as a result of universal tendencies that have been making the functioning of the system more uniform across the board, nation-states have virtually dissolved and national sovereignty has lost its meaning."

But the opposite is the case, Balaguer pointed out. "Globalization does not imply an automatic mechanism for solving the contradictions and unevennesses that have accompanied the development of capitalism." A new level of interimperialist rivalry, and the widening of the gap between the developed and underdeveloped countries and within them, means that the world is today "more unstable, more prone to disintegration, and more politically explosive than ever."

A work group of four Cuban participants from the University of Havana and the research department of the party Central Committee took up the discussion on this theme in the commission on imperialism. In their summary remarks they argued that the monopoly state capitalism of Lenin's time, on which his analysis of imperialism was based, has today "metamorphosed" into transnational capitalism. As capital circulates more and more massively across borders, they insisted, it "increasingly abandons any national basis."

The debate on this theme and its political implications continued on and off over the three days. One of the clearest replies came from another of the Cuban participants in the commission, Central Committee member Jorge Risquet Valdés. Risquet used his two-minute intervention to refute the implication that major capitalist enterprises no longer depend on one or another state to defend their property and interests. "Big capital still needs a state," Risquet replied. "With their growing crisis, each capitalist power—now more than ever—needs an army against its foreign competitors and a police force against its own working class."

To confront the power of imperialism, he emphasized, revolutionists need to take and wield state power, as they have done in Cuba. He reminded participants in the conference that he was speaking on October 22, 35 years to the day since the U.S. government brought the world to the brink of nuclear war and threatened the annihilation of the entire Cuban people over the issue of Soviet missiles that were installed in Cuba in an act of sovereign self-defense.

Other delegates, speaking for the Socialist Workers Party in the United States and the National Democratic Front of South Korea, also replied to the political implications of the position that "globalization" represents something qualitatively new in the history of capitalism and that nation-states have diminished importance in today's world.

The south Korean delegate reminded participants of the 37,000 U.S. troops stationed in his country and the permanent threat of war their presence brings.

Rectification

In the commission on Realities of Contemporary Socialism, a discussion unfolded around the character of the rectification process that was initiated by the leadership of the Cuban Communist Party in 1986. Manuel Monereo, education secretary of the Communist Party of Spain, and a member of the federal leadership of the Izquierda Unida (United Left), questioned the assessment put forward by Darío Machado, director of the Havana-based Center for the Study of the Americas, who explained that Cuba had been able to confront the challenge of the special period following the collapse of the Soviet bloc, because of measures taken during the rectification process that had strengthened the revolution. The spirit of internationalist missions had been brought home, voluntary work brigades expanded, and the involvement of workers in making decisions on production deepened, Machado said.

Monereo challenged this assessment, asking whether rectification and volunteer work brigades had not in fact exacerbated the economic problems Cuba faced because of their "inefficiency," and argued that there was nothing inherently revolutionary in involving workers in production decisions—that is what Toyota does to increase productivity.

Machado had presented a report that expanded on another of the themes in Balaguer's opening remarks.

Noting that at this conference he had "no desire to spend time in an analysis of the collapse of socialism" in Europe, Balaguer called attention to the fact that "the so-called domino effect" did not extend to Cuba. "The liquidation of socialism in Eastern Europe and the USSR had its historic, socioeconomic, and political causes, which we have been clarifying among ourselves," he remarked. "But one thing has been well demonstrated: that European process did not mean the failure of socialism as a system."

Nor did it imply, Balaguer continued, "that Marxism and Leninism are useless as guides for our actions. It did mean the crumbling of a dogmatic and vulgar type of Marxism, which in those countries came to hold the strength of an official theory, burying many of the central principles of our classics and elevating to the position of universal law certain theses that only served to justify political positions and that had barely any scientific basis."

We all know, Balaguer added, "that the classics did not present us a blueprint of the socialist society; rather they elaborated fundamental theses. The socialism that succumbed had been moving away from the socialist ideal envisioned by Marx, Engels, Lenin, and other Marxists."

As that was happening, Balaguer noted, "Cuba was going through a process of rectification of errors and negative tendencies initiated in 1986 by the leadership of our party. We had arrived at the conclusion that the model of economic management, copied in large measure from the Soviet experience, had to be deeply transformed," because it had "diverted the construction of socialism into paths that were in no way revolutionary."

"We began a process on a social scale, which started in the economic arena and spread to the political life of the country. We began a process of rectification and perfecting of our socialism, based on socialist positions."

GRANMA

Capitalist crisis will lead to further slaughters of working people like U.S.-led war against people of Iraq in 1991, **above.** To confront imperialism, Balaguer stressed, revolutionists need to take and wield state power. He was speaking 35 years after Washington brought the world to the brink of nuclear war over Soviet missiles in Cuba, installed in self-defense. **Below,** Cuban militia members with antiaircraft guns in front of Hotel Riviera in Havana during October 1962 missile crisis.

In answering the challenge to rectification raised by the representative of the Communist Party of Spain in the commission discussion, Machado insisted that the involvement of Cuban working people in solving the basic economic and social problems they confronted—as the workers parliaments during the special period had done—meant recovering the most "indigenous" element of the Cuban revolution.

Alliances, principles, and the ranks

A third discussion, and one with even more direct political consequences throughout the world, took place informally around the question of what kinds of alliances revolutionists should negotiate with other political parties that oppose capitalist austerity offensives (and the temporary relationship of forces that make them possible) often referred to, throughout Latin America especially, as "neoliberalism." This strategic question too had been raised by Balaguer in his keynote remarks.

Because of the "increasing transfer of sovereignty and decision-making toward the centers of world power and the transnational bodies," Balaguer noted, "state power, one of the objectives that revolutionary struggles are fought over, begins to be undervalued. That is why it is a priority to reassess the question of struggles for power, as well as the instruments and forms of political participation by the left in society."

In pursuing a policy of alliances in response to capitalist policies aimed at driving down the wages and living standards of working people and at curtailing democratic rights, Balaguer argued, "in our opinion, an agreement of revolutionary forces with other sectors around short-, medium-, or long-term objectives should be a process in which the parties put forward their own essential interests with total clarity. It does not seem acceptable to renounce socialism or revolutionary positions in order to be accepted. . . . The one thing that is not negotiable is principles."

Balaguer also stressed the importance of non-exclusion—not reproducing "on other levels the old traditions of sectarianism that leave us so vulnerable in the face of imperialist domination." The great diversity of new social forces, along with the reshaping of others, he noted, creates new possibilities for a broad policy of alliances involving environmentalists, peasants, those without land or without a roof over their heads, forces organized against gender, religious, racial, or ethnic oppression, and others.

Alliances negotiated as deals between leaders without the support and understanding of the rank and file, moreover, are unacceptable from a revolutionary standpoint, Balaguer noted. "The essence of any alliance that claims to have a left perspective is that it be structured from, by, and for the ranks," he emphasized.

Although it did not come to the workshop floor in an explicit manner, it was clear from several days of informal discussions with delegates that debates and divisions over such questions have cut deeply into centrist political regroupments such as the Workers Party of Brazil. They also pose major challenges for revolutionary forces.

Despite suggestions from a few delegates that it would be good to draft a common political statement to be adopted at the conclusion of the three days of discussion, the conference hosts and the overwhelming majority of participants insisted that the importance of the gathering was the fact that it had initiated a process of discussion that, together with events like the youth festival and trade union gathering, should be pursued in coming months, in various journals and conferences as appropriate. The workshop concluded with a consensus among the majority of those present, however, that the initiative to bring together such an international gathering of political parties could not have come from any quarter other than the Communist Party of Cuba and that it represented an important watershed.

As Balaguer expressed it, "we have not the slightest doubt that the world has the choice of two roads: either the continuation of capitalist barbarism or the search for alternatives to this stage. For us Cubans, as for millions of human beings, the alternative continues to be socialism."

Marcella FitzGerald and Michel Prairie contributed to this article.

CUBAN PARTY CONGRESS STRENGTHENS SOCIALIST COURSE OF REVOLUTION

by Martín Koppel and Mary-Alice Waters

HAVANA—"We are open to all options and all experiences—all except surrendering, except giving up socialism, except renouncing the gains of the revolution and the power held by the people, except allowing others to be the masters of our country." Affirmation of this fundamental political course was at the center of Cuban president Fidel Castro's opening report to the Fifth Congress of the Communist Party of Cuba, held here October 8–10.

GRANMA

GRANMA

Cuban president Fidel Castro **(right)** gives opening report to fifth congress of Communist Party of Cuba, on October 8. Congress delegates approve resolution **(above)**. Portraits on stage depict (from left to right) Karl Marx, founder of modern communist movement; Bolshevik party leader V.I. Lenin; José Martí, Cuba's national hero; Julio Antonio Mella, founder of the Cuban Communist Party in 1925; and Ernesto Che Guevara. Slogan on stage says, "These people, this party, will never surrender their unity. Fidel."

It was confirmed by the almost 1,500 delegates attending the gathering and was voiced repeatedly both in the congress discussion and on the street by working people who followed the deliberations on television and radio, which broadcast many hours of coverage.

The party congress "focused on the question we have all been discussing—the economy," said Juan José Iglesias, 51, a worker from a paint factory here. "Fidel was right in what he said. To get out of the 'Special Period' there are no recipes or miracles. We have to keep fighting, working very hard, relying on the intelligence and creativity of every human being. What we won't do is go back to the old days of capitalism."

Iglesias made this comment as he stood in line with 60 of his co-workers and thousands of other people at the Plaza of the Revolution to pay tribute to Ernesto Che Guevara and his fellow revolutionaries who fell in battle in Bolivia 30 years ago (see accompanying article below). He was referring to the severe economic crisis in Cuba—known here as the Special Period—precipitated in 1990 by the abrupt loss of some 85 percent of the small island nation's foreign trade as the Soviet bloc regimes disintegrated.

The congress itself opened on the date commemorated as the 30th anniversary of Che's murder by the U.S.-backed Bolivian military. It closed on October 10, anniversary of *El grito de Yara* (the Cry of Yara), the call to arms that launched Cuba's

Reprinted from *Militant* vol. 61, no. 37, Oct. 27, 1997.

first war of independence from Spain in 1868.

Delegates to the fifth congress adopted four major resolutions: a document titled "The party of unity, democracy and the human rights we defend"; a resolution on economic policy; a resolution approving the line of the main report given by Castro; and modifications to the party's statutes. They also elected a Central Committee, the decision-making body between congresses, and ratified the Political Bureau and the first and second secretaries elected by the new Central Committee.

The Communist Party had published and circulated "The party of unity, democracy and the human rights we defend" shortly after the congress was called in mid-April. The document was discussed over the past months by party members, members of the Union of Young Communists (UJC), and in thousands of meetings at workplaces and neighborhoods, organized by the trade unions and other mass organizations.

The document traces Cuba's revolutionary legacy—from the 19th century battles for independence from Spain, to the struggles against U.S. imperialist domination throughout the 20th century, to the 1959 revolutionary overthrow of the U.S.-backed Batista dictatorship—and reviews the gains of the socialist revolution. Answering the arguments by opponents of the revolution that the Cuban government and Communist Party are totalitarian, it defends the democratic character of Cuba's socialist revolution as one in which working people hold state power.

Concrete discussion on economy

The heart of the congress deliberations was a concrete discussion of the severe economic crisis Cuba has lived through since the last party congress took place in 1991, and a reaffirmation of the determination to find a collective, working-class road forward.

This discussion began with the opening report by Fidel Castro, the party's first secretary. Castro put aside the written report that had been prepared for him to read to the congress, and simply spoke to the delegates—and through them to the Cuban people—for almost seven hours. He detailed the conditions that Cuba has faced and dealt with over the past six years.

Between 1989 and 1992, Castro noted, Cuba's imports had dropped from roughly $8 billion a year to one quarter that amount. "What a brutal and sudden drop this was in food and other basic necessities of life for the country, for 10 million people, for the revolution."

By 1992, Cuba had lost most vital sources of supplies and markets, and had to look for new ones, the Cuban president said. "Hundreds of thousands of men and women were left practically with no work or raw materials in the factories. The amount of paper money in circulation expanded to startling proportions. Our currency was tremendously devalued. State subsidies expanded. The budget deficit grew, reaching 30 percent or more of the Gross Domestic Product." Castro added that even arms supplies and other defense-related equipment for Cuba's Revolutionary Armed Forces shrank to zero.

Given this drastic picture, made even more critical by Washington's economic war against Cuba, which time and again torpedoed new painstakingly negotiated trade agreements, capitalist spokespeople around the world "predicted the revolution's days were numbered. They predicted this small country would be unable to stand up to the United States," Castro noted.

But what did they think we were we going to do? he asked. "Go down on our knees? Surrender? . . . That's what they demanded of Cuba: unconditional surrender, turning over the entire nation and people to the enemies of the nation and people, renouncing our gains, ideas, and ideals."

The Cuban revolutionary leadership took a different course, Castro said. They rejected going back to "the indignities of the past." In doing so, Castro noted, they have also had to wage a fight inside the country "against those who become disheartened, demoralized, those who have no principles, those who break laws at the expense of everyone else."

Refuse to go back to capitalism

Castro reviewed some of the most important measures taken to reverse the economic free fall and to revive production, such as allowing use of the U.S. dollar as a legal currency, developing tourism and encouraging foreign capitalist investment in Cuba. "Although we did not like this very much, development required capital, it required seeking new technology and markets," he said.

These measures, the Cuban leader noted, have inevitably generated undesirable social differences. He went on to say that despite these negative consequences Cuba has been able to maintain the most basic conquests of the revolution. The plunge in the Gross Domestic Product bottomed out in 1994 and since then a slight economic recovery has been under way.

In contrast to "other countries that live in a permanent Special Period," Castro said, Cuba still has social indices such as life expectancy and infant mortality that are comparable to those of the industrialized nations.

He referred to the rise in infant mortality, decline in life expectancy, and other deteriorating aspects of life in the former Soviet Union. He said this demonstrated what it means to renounce a socialist course and follow a road toward capitalism, "a system that, while dominant, is prehistoric because it has nothing to offer humanity—a wolf trying to devour another wolf has nothing to do with human beings."

Washington is waging a full-fledged economic war against Cuba, Castro stressed. "That's why we must be soldiers and fight like good soldiers in the economic war." He emphasized the need for political leadership to fight these battles, noting that "special work is needed for the education of youth."

'Che and revolution are same thing'

Castro devoted the whole final part of his speech to the importance of Che Guevara's leadership qualities, his ideas, the role Guevara played in Cuba and the identity between Che and the Cuban revolution. Che and Cubans came together on the *Granma,* Castro explained, to begin the revolutionary war. Together they lived through the October crisis in 1962 when Washington threatened to annihilate the Cuban people in a nuclear confrontation. Together "they began the construction of socialism, this socialism that is as much ours as his." And together they fought and died in Africa and Bolivia. "Che and the revolution are the same thing," he declared.

The major discussion at the congress took place under the report on the draft Economic Resolution, which was given by Political Bureau member Carlos Lage, who is also secretary of the Executive Committee of the Council of Ministers. Despite increases in areas such as nickel production, light industry, construction materials, and tobacco—signs of the recovery—the Cuban economy has grown by only 2.1 percent so far this year. Last year's growth was 7.8 percent.

The main cause of the lower economic growth, Lage noted, was the fall in sugar production. While no official figures have been released on the size of this year's sugar production, the most common estimate is 4.2 million tons, down from last year's level of 4.45 million tons. In comparison, for several years immediately prior to the beginning of the Special Period, annual sugar production ran close to 8 million tons.

The biggest blow to this year's sugar harvest was the loss of $200 million in financing due to the U.S. government's implementation of the so-called Helms-Burton act. This law mandates sanctions against companies "trafficking" in property formerly owned by U.S. citizens in Cuba. The Cuban government lost these short-term, high-interest loans at the crucial time needed to finance imports of fertilizer, spare machine parts, and other supplies for the harvest.

Lage highlighted some of the problems facing the Basic Units of Cooperative Production (UBPCs), both those growing sugarcane and those producing food crops. According to the figures released in late September, at the National Conference of Non-Sugarcane UBPCs in Santiago de Cuba, some 69 percent of the non-sugarcane UBPCs in Cuba are operating at a loss, although overall it is a smaller loss than a year ago. Barely one out of four of these co-ops is self-sufficient in food today. These problems are even more critical in the cane-growing UBPCs.

The Cuban government began the transformation of the country's state farms into smaller cooperative units four years ago. In these UBPCs, which account for 42 percent of the arable land, cooperative members have the right to use the land and own the fruit of their labor.

The challenge in agriculture

The richest part of the congress discussion focused on the crisis in agriculture today. Numerous delegates gave clear and concrete assessments of the challenges faced, and in some cases described ex-

GRANMA/ISMAEL FRANCISCO MILITANT/LAURA GARZA

Ramón Romero **(left, at microphone)**, president of the Primer Soviet de América sugarcane-producing cooperative in Mabay, Granma province, tells delegates how the farm has consistently obtained good yields for the last 14 years. Standing behind Romero is Orlando Lugo Fonte, president of the National Association of Small Farmers (ANAP). The richest part of the congress discussion focused on the crisis in Cuba's agriculture today and perspectives for overcoming it. **Right,** workers harvest sugarcane at cooperative in Santa Clara, March 1996.

amples where workers and farmers had made important advances. The thread running throughout the discussion, as Castro emphasized in his report, was that there are no magical solutions, that what is needed is communist leadership to eradicate administrative, routinist methods, combined with just plain hard work.

Ramón Romero, president of the Primer Soviet de América (First Soviet of America) sugarcane-producing cooperative in Mabay, Granma province, described with a wealth of detail how the farmers there had consistently obtained good yields for the past 14 years. The Primer Soviet is a kind of cooperative, known as Agricultural Production Cooperative (CPA), that was organized much earlier than the UBPCs.

Romero explained their careful attention to cane varieties used, efforts to reduce costs, the active involvement of all members of the co-op, and the resulting high morale. They also work an average of 10 hours a day, he said, whereas the average on many newly formed UBPCs is reported to be closer to 5 hours a day.

The presidents of 39 other CPAs from provinces across Cuba have traveled to the Primer Soviet, Orlando Lugo Fonte, president of the National Association of Small Farmers (ANAP), told delegates, taking that experience back with them to generalize the example. Part of the discussion by congress delegates was on the role the Cuban army has played in helping increase agricultural production through the Youth Army of Labor (EJT).

The EJT, volunteer units of young army recruits, often takes on farms that are the most difficult challenge. They work alongside the civilian workers and set high standards of discipline and productivity.

Róger Delgado, from Matanzas, recounted the experience at the Victoria de Girón (Girón Victory) citrus orchard in Jagüey Grande, of which he is the director. On this farm, organized by the EJT, workers produced 400,000 tons of fruit in the last year, breaking their historic record set in 1989, before the Special Period. They did so with only half the cultivated land, fewer tractors, and less fuel consumption. They organize two daily shifts and have taken other steps to improve their efficiency.

Belén Peña, 37, from Santiago province, is the president of a coffee farm belonging to the Naranjal UBPC, as well as secretary of the Communist Party nucleus at that farm. She related how workers there had completely turned around coffee production on the farm, transforming it from the worst in the municipality to the best. Then she sparked surprise, laughter, and applause, when she described how she and other workers had replaced the entire executive board, including the UBPC administrator—who is her husband, she told the congress—for "cronyism."

Discussion on UBPC cooperatives

At the request of the congress presiding committee, several provincial Communist Party secretaries in major sugar-producing provinces addressed the political problems behind the economic difficulties faced on the UBPCs. Pedro Sáez, party first secretary in Sancti Spíritu, stated, "When the state farms were turned into UBPCs, many of the directors of the state farms went on to become presidents of UBPCs. There was no change in mentality—they still had the idea that there were limitless resources and no consequences."

Similarly, Jorge Luis Sierra, first secretary in Holguín province, said that in the reorganization of state farms "the structures changed but the cadres didn't."

The first secretary in Santiago province, Juan Carlos Robinson, argued that if there is no discipline, even a considerable productive potential will be frittered away. Other key factors, he stressed, are the use of the workday and the political leadership by the local party unit. In Santiago province, one of those that has registered real gains, "we have 100 percent of the cane-producing areas planted—there are no unused areas; that makes a big difference."

Leadership question

One of the most important points on the congress agenda was the election of the Central Committee. Raúl Castro, second secretary of the party, reported on the work of the commission that made nominations for the new body. The congress decided to elect a new Central Committee of 150, one-third smaller than the previous one. Castro explained that the last two congresses had elected a committee of 225, eliminating the category of candidate CC members. He said the committee had become overly large and that many did not really function as part of a collective working body.

In arguing for the size reduction, Raúl Castro pointed out that the Chinese Communist Party has a Central Committee of 300-plus even though the party membership is 58 million—compared with some 600,000 members of the Cuban Communist Party. The Central Committee, he argued, should not be based on representation, but on demonstrated leadership capacities.

He noted that "there exists a perception that someone who comes off the Central Committee will never be returned" to the CC, but that this is false.

Castro also spoke about the need for renewal and continuing the transition in leadership. The election of the Central Committee was seen by many as a way to advance this transition toward an increasingly experienced generation of Cuban leaders that grew up within the revolution.

The new committee includes a number of younger party cadres, including a significant number who were formerly central leaders of the UJC and are today taking on major day-to-day party and government leadership responsibilities.

The Political Bureau of 24 was also renewed. The six members who have not previously served on it include some of the younger provincial party secretaries, such as Sáez, Robinson, and Sierra, and Misael Enamorado from Las Tunas.

Of the congress delegates themselves, 16 percent were under the age of 35. Some 22 percent were women.

In a major speech closing the congress, Fidel Castro returned to the main political questions discussed. He emphasized the positive examples that delegates had described of working people taking control of decisions and organizing themselves to make gains in raising production while holding down costs.

In each case, there was nothing mysterious or unique about the reasons for their success, he noted. "We must turn the exceptions into the rule, we must turn efficiency into the rule."

Castro pointed out that in the name of efficiency, capitalists and their governments carry out policies against the interests of working people. "We are not going to privatize companies—we will not take that road," he said. In capitalist countries such moves have led to layoffs and speedup on the job. In a country where workers and farmers hold power, the struggle for efficiency and quality and against waste must be part of working people taking increasing control of the country's economy for the benefit of humanity.

'We can do it better than capitalists'

"If capitalists can manage a company efficiently, we socialists can do so better than the capitalists," Castro argued. "We have the obligation to become administrators, good administrators. Let us do it not only for our well-being. Let us do it for the beautiful ideas that we are defending [and] to fight this unsustainable and ruthless capitalist system that has no future."

In the early years of the Cuban revolution, "we had the spirit of 'Homeland or Death, We Shall Win.' " Now, Castro added, "we must have that same spirit" in fighting to improve productivity.

Castro returned in his closing speech to the kind of leadership working people need. He underlined the capacity of human beings to transform themselves through revolutionary struggle, pointing to the thousands of Cubans who have taken part in internationalist missions in countries like Nicaragua and Angola. "This is what Che meant when he said that being a revolutionary is the highest expression of humanity," he emphasized.

Castro recalled the life of Roberto Rodríguez, a combatant in the Rebel Army better known as El Vaquerito (Little Cowboy) who rapidly became an outstanding fighter in Guevara's Column 8 and a leader of the celebrated "Suicide Squad," which took on some of the most dangerous military assignments. He was killed in Santa Clara on Dec. 30, 1958, on the eve of the revolutionary victory.

"Vaquerito himself could not have imagined what he became. Humans have more capacities than what people think, and our duty as communists is to discover, promote, and develop those qualities. That was Che's virtue—his ability to promote these capacities, mainly by his own example.

"Now, when we are commemorating the 30th anniversary of his death, we must bring back something more than his mortal remains. We must also bring back his immortal ideas and example."

GREETINGS FROM THE SOCIALIST WORKERS PARTY NATIONAL COMMITTEE TO THE FIFTH CONGRESS OF THE COMMUNIST PARTY OF CUBA

Below are the greetings sent by Socialist Workers Party National Secretary Jack Barnes for the party's National Committee to the Fifth Congress of the Communist Party that took place in Havana, Cuba, October 8–10. Reprinted from *Militant* vol. 61, No. 36, Oct. 20, 1997.

Dear Comrades,

Commemoration of the 30th anniversary of the fall in combat of the Heroic Guerrilla and his comrades not only solemnly marks the 5th Congress of the Communist Party in Cuba and reminds us all of the course that Fidel has fought for from the beginning. It also foreshadows the battles that will decide the fate of the 21st century.

New generations of revolutionary toilers—including those inside the most brutal and mighty imperialist power in history, the United States of America—will draw strength from the example of these heroic fighters and the lessons we have learned from the men and women who made the Cuban revolution possible and changed the course of history in our time.

The reality that will mark the century on whose threshold we stand is that of the growing historic weakness of U.S. imperialism—faced as it is around the world with ever increasing numbers of gravediggers of its own creation, and diminishing political barriers to unity in struggle amongst them. As that truth breaks through the surface of imperialist wealth and arrogance, the example of the combatants of Ñacahuazú, of the leadership of the Sierra Maestra, and of the worker-bolsheviks who established and defended the first socialist victory in our century will be emulated.

Our task is to organize, prepare, and fight—now.

Communist greetings,
Jack Barnes
NATIONAL SECRETARY
FOR THE NATIONAL COMMITTEE OF THE SOCIALIST WORKERS PARTY

CUBAN GENERALS DISCUSS RECORD OF REVOLUTIONARY ARMED FORCES

by Argiris Malapanis and Mary-Alice Waters

The following is a review of *Secretos de Generales* (Secrets of the Generals), by Luis Báez; Si-Mar Publishing, 1996; Havana, Cuba; 546 pp.; in Spanish.

HAVANA—"Where did you serve on your first mission as an internationalist?" Cuban journalist Luis Báez asks Ulises Rosales del Toro, division general of Cuba's Revolutionary Armed Forces (FAR) and chief of staff of the FAR.

"In October 1963, in Algeria, as chief of staff of the Tactical Combat Group during the war Morocco launched at the border with the goal of forcibly annexing sections of Algerian territory," the Cuban general says.

The Algerians had recently gained their independence from France, Rosales del Toro continues. "They had just began to govern the country, and their armed forces had not been fully formed. For these reasons they were at a disadvantage in confronting Morocco, which enjoyed the support of the great powers. Faced with this situation, Algerian president [Ahmed] Ben Bella asked for Cuba's help."

Algerian people celebrate newly won independence from France in 1962. Cuban volunteers responded to request for aid from the revolutionary government in Algiers, when the Moroccan regime, supported by imperialist powers, attacked Algeria in 1963. Ulises Rosales del Toro **(inset)**, former Chief of Staff of Cuba's Revolutionary Armed Forces (FAR), was among the Cuban revolutionaries who did a tour of duty in Algeria at the time. He was 21 years old then. In October 1997 Rosales del Toro was appointed head of the Ministry of Sugar. Gen. Alvaro López Viera was named Chief of Staff of the FAR.

"What do you draw from your experiences?" asks Báez.

"It was my first trip abroad and my initial contact with the revolutionary movement in another country," says Rosales. He was 21 years old then.

"At the time, Algeria was a school for African revolutionaries. You could see African combatants there preparing to go and fight for national independence in their countries. . . . In addition, I got to know the poverty and the social difficulties facing the Algerian people, who, just like us, had begun the process of building a new society.

"I also saw our FAR operate as a combat unit, engaging in action, maintaining a high level of cohesiveness and preparedness to fight far away from our country. It was an unforgettable experience.

"I stayed in Algeria until May 1964," Rosales says. "Our unit did not engage in combat. But our determination to do so and our presence in the middle

Reprinted from *Militant* vol. 61, no. 21, May 26, 1997.

of a war zone was of great importance to me."

The interview with Rosales concludes the book *Secrets of the Generals*, published here in Cuba earlier this year.

The book comprises 41 interviews with the top military officers of Cuba's armed forces. Báez is a veteran journalist for the Cuban news agency Prensa Latina.

As Raúl Castro, minister of the FAR, says in his preface, *Secrets of the Generals* "is not a textbook on the past, but living history. It is an opportunity to share 41 stories of the Cuban epic in the second half of this century." The book, he says, will contribute to passing on "to new generations the treasure of moral values and accumulated combat experience."

Forty-one stories

These stories are told by 26 brigadier generals, 13 division generals, one army corps general, and one vice admiral of the navy. The officers explain who they are and how they joined the revolutionary movement. They talk about their experiences around the world as they fought alongside national liberation movements in Africa, Asia, and Latin America.

Many, like Rosales, come from peasant families, or working-class backgrounds. Some learned to read and write only after the triumph of the revolution.

Like Rosales, most took part in the revolutionary war in the Sierra Maestra mountains of eastern Cuba. That war, launched in December 1956 by the July 26 Movement and Rebel Army under the leadership of Fidel Castro, toppled the U.S.-backed tyranny of Fulgencio Batista on New Year's Day in 1959.

Thirty three of the officers interviewed fought with the Rebel Army, and five joined the FAR after the triumph of the revolution. The remaining three had been officers in the Cuban army who opposed the Batista dictatorship and participated in attempts to organize coups against it.

The FAR was forged out of the men and women who fought in the Sierra Maestra.

Book attracts attention

Secrets of the Generals has generated considerable interest in Cuba. The small first printing immediately sold out. In recent weeks *Granma*, the main Cuban daily, the weekly *Juventud Rebelde* (Rebel Youth), and other Cuban newspapers have run several of the interviews published in *Secrets*. The Cuban weekly *Granma International* ran a review of the book in its March 26 issue. At the end of last year, Cuban television broadcast a 17-part series of documentaries on episodes from the revolution's history, based on narrations by many of the same generals Báez interviewed.

The book has also caught the attention of some media in the United States, especially the Spanish-language press. The *Miami Herald* and its sister publication in Spanish, *El Nuevo Herald*, ran reviews of the book in March as did the Los Angeles-based Spanish-language daily *La Opinión*. These articles zero in on the comments by the Cuban generals regarding the internationalist missions in which they participated.

Moncada and Bayamo

Brigadier general Calíxto García, 66 years old today, participated in the July 26, 1953, attack on the Bayamo garrison, one of the very first battles against the Batista dictatorship. The assault was carried out simultaneously with the attack on the nearby Moncada barracks, the main army garrison in Santiago de Cuba, by 160 revolutionaries under the command of Fidel Castro. The combatants did not succeed in taking the garrisons and over 50 were captured and murdered. Another 28 were tried, convicted and imprisoned; they were pardoned in 1955 in response to a massive amnesty campaign.

But the assault on Moncada launched the insurrection against Batista. Out of that action and the subsequent political campaign to free the imprisoned combatants the July 26 Movement was born.

García escaped arrest in Bayamo and managed to get out of the country. He spent almost a year in Costa Rica and Honduras before making his way to Mexico, where he was later reunited with Fidel Castro and other revolutionaries.

While in San José, Costa Rica, he says, "I became friends with Che Guevara, whom I used to see at the Soda Palace, a cafe at the center of the city where many exiles used to meet at all hours of the night. . . . I think I was the first to talk to Che about Fidel, Cuba, and our July 26 Movement."

Ernesto Che Guevara, Argentinian by birth, joined the Cuban rebels in Mexico and became one of the central leaders of the Cuban revolution.

García took part in the landing of the *Granma*, the yacht that transported Castro, Guevara, and the other fighters from Mexico to eastern Cuba, where they began the revolutionary war in the Sierra Maestra in late 1956. By the end of the war, García was a commander of the Rebel Army. He later served as a member of the Central Committee of the Communist Party from 1965 to 1980. He is now retired from the FAR.

Prison rebellion

One of the most interesting accounts in the book is the story of the prison break-out that coincided with the Granma landing. It is told by Raúl Menéndez Tomassevich, known as Tomás, who is today a division general.

While a teenager, Tomás worked as a messenger in Rubio, a factory that produced rope-soled shoes in Santiago de Cuba. In 1952 he was imprisoned for "a common crime," as he puts it, "for counterfeiting official documents. I falsified the signature of the mayor of Santiago de Cuba, Felipe Fernández Castillo, in order to withdraw a bunch of pesos from his bank account."

In the Boniato prison, Tomás solidarized with a hunger strike by the revolutionaries who had carried out the assault on Moncada, many of whom were jailed in that same penitentiary for a while. As a result of that action, he was locked in solitary confinement for 50 days. In jail, Tomás met and talked with leaders of the July 26 Movement, becoming a firm supporter. After four years of imprisonment, he organized a prison break-out that was coordinated with strikes and demonstrations called by the July 26 Movement to coincide with the Granma landing.

Tomás, two other prisoners convicted of common crimes, and four leaders of the July 26 Movement escaped "at seven o'clock in the morning, after disarming various policemen, soldiers, and prison officials." The break-out, he says, was authorized by July 26 Movement leader Frank País and was carried out on Nov. 30, 1956. "That same day the actions in Santiago to support Fidel's landing took place as well."

Tomás then became an active member of the clandestine movement against Batista in Santiago. One of his tasks was working in an underground facility making grenades. He later joined the rebels in the Sierra Maestra, rising to the rank of Rebel Army commander. In 1961 and 1962, he served as chief of operations against the bandits in the Escambray mountains, organized by the CIA, who carried out a guerrilla campaign against the revolution. Later he took part in training the combatants who went with Guevara to Bolivia. In 1966 and 1967, Tomás took part in internationalist missions in the Portuguese African colony of Guinea Bissau and in Venezuela, and subsequently in Angola.

The story of the Boniato jail break-out is described in greater detail by Menéndez in the book *Prison Rebellion*, written together with José Gárciga Blanco, a lt. colonel of the FAR. A launching of this book, just published by Editora Política, was held in Havana April 25.

In another account in *Secrets of the Generals*, Delsa Esther Puebla Viltre describes how young women took leadership responsibility and acquired combat experience in the Sierra Maestra, overcoming strong initial objections by several commanders. Puebla, now a brigadier general of the FAR, was the first woman to rise to this rank in Cuba's Revolutionary Armed Forces.

First major defeat of U.S. empire

The revolutionary struggle against Batista reverberated within the dictator's army, and a number of officers were involved in various military coup conspiracies. A few were won to the side of the revolution and played important roles in building the Revolutionary Armed Forces.

Enrique Carreras Rolas, now division general of the FAR, had been an officer in Batista's air force. After agreeing to participate in a military plot against the regime in mid-1957, he was jailed by the dictatorship and remained in prison until the triumph of the revolution. In early 1959, Carreras was named head of the revolutionary air force, which at that point had only a handful of fighter planes and only three pilots with any combat experience. He began training classes for new pilots, held at the military base of San Antonio de los Baños, in Havana province. Washington had built the base in the 1940s in order to refuel its planes flying to and from South America, Carreras says.

PHOTOS COURTESY OF GRANMA

Cuban soldiers at Playa Girón after defeat of U.S.-organized mercenaries, April 19, 1961 **(above)**. José Ramón Fernández **(at center of photo on right)**, chief of military operations at Playa Girón and brigadier general of the FAR today, inspects some of the weapons captured from mercenary forces at Bay of Pigs, April 1961.

"I can tell you, without fear of contradiction, that the revolutionary combat air force was born and created at that air base in San Antonio de los Baños," he notes.

Carreras, like most generals interviewed in the book, is a veteran of the Playa Girón battle in 1961, usually called the Bay of Pigs in the United States. That's when the popular militias and the Revolutionary Armed Forces inflicted a crushing defeat on the U.S.-organized mercenaries who invaded Cuba in a failed attempt to overthrow the workers and peasants regime. In a recent speech on the 36th anniversary of this historic battle, Raúl Castro described its outcome as "the first great military defeat inflicted on the United States on this continent."

During the mercenary invasion, Carreras notes, "the enemy forces had approximately a 5–1 advantage on planes and a 12–1 advantage on pilots."

The small, ill-equipped, and newly trained Cuban air force played a central role in the defeat of the counterrevolutionaries. "In less than 72 hours, 10 pilots with eight dilapidated planes flew 70 missions," Carreras explains. Between April 17 and April 19, 1961, Carreras and the other Cuban pilots downed nine B-26 bombers. "We also sank two army transport ships, three LCT boats carrying tanks, and five landing boats." In bringing down the enemy planes, the Cubans killed 14 counterrevolutionaries, including four U.S. instructors.

Later, Carreras headed a Cuban air force mission to Vietnam during Washington's war against the Vietnamese people that also ended with the defeat of U.S. imperialism in 1975.

How *tanquistas* were trained

Division general Néstor López Cuba completed a training course on operating tanks at the Managua military camp near Havana in 1959 and stayed on at the school as an instructor.

In face of mounting military threats and economic pressure from Washington, the new Cuban government began receiving aid from abroad, López Cuba explains in the book. "In October 1960 Soviet technical aid began arriving," he tells Báez. "They said it came from Czechoslovakia, but the T-34's and SAU-100's were Russian tanks.

"Commander Guillermo García asked me to select the best graduates of the two courses on American tanks we had just completed and organize classes on operating the Soviet tanks. I picked 22 graduates. . . . It was a very intense period of training. Everything we learned in the morning from the Soviet instructors we had to teach at night to the rest of the compañeros using whatever tools we had at our disposal. . . .

"In February [1961] we carried out combat practice in Guanito, Pinar del Rio. With that exercise we finished the first course on Soviet tanks."

The newly trained *tanquistas,* led by López Cuba and other officers of the FAR, were essential in crushing the mercenary invaders at Playa Girón.

Another officer who describes the events leading up to and during the Bay of Pigs invasion is brigadier general José Ramón Fernández Álvarez, today vice president of Cuba's Council of Ministers.

Fernández was part of a revolt by officers in Batista's army, called *Los Puros* (the pure ones), on April 4, 1956, for which he was imprisoned. "Among the officers in that group, I was the most radical," Fernández says. "I thought we had to arrest Batista and execute him for his responsibility in the killings of thousands of people. I had proposed that we needed to carry out an agrarian reform, purge the armed forces, implement the 1940 constitution, and confiscate the goods stolen by public officials. That's as far as I got at the time."

The big majority of inmates incarcerated with Fernández at the infamous Isle of Pines prison were members of the July 26 Movement, and they had a big impact on him. Fernández joined the revolutionary movement after Batista was toppled and was chief of military operations at the Bay of Pigs battle.

Fernández says he went to Playa Girón with great enthusiasm. Even though he had rebelled against Batista, he tells Báez, "I hadn't had the opportunity—as the compañeros who fought in the Sierra [mountains] and the llano [plains] did—to put my life in danger to demonstrate the justice of the ideas we believed in.

"Girón meant for me putting my own body on the line in defense of the revolution and socialism."

Internationalist missions

Army Corps General Abelardo Colomé Ibarra, known as "Furry," participated in the clandestine struggle against the Batista dictatorship in Santiago de Cuba and joined the Rebel Army in 1957 at age 17. Like many others, he comes from a working-class family. His mother was a worker in a biscuit factory and his father was a cook. Today he is a member of the Political Bureau of the Communist Party of Cuba and minister of the interior.

In 1962, Colomé left Cuba for an internationalist mission in Argentina and Bolivia that lasted two years. The goal of the expedition was "to prepare the conditions for a guerrilla uprising in Argentina that would be headed by journalist Jorge Ricardo Masetti, who had developed strong ties with his compatriot Ernesto Che Guevara," Colomé says.

"At the time I was 22 years old. Considering my age, I was given tremendous responsibility. I had to travel in the area several times to study and prepare the terrain."

Masetti had gone to Cuba's Sierra Maestra in January 1958 and joined the revolutionary movement there. After the triumph, he became founding director of Prensa Latina, the press service launched by the new revolutionary government in Havana.

Masetti was killed in 1964 while leading the guerrilla nucleus he helped launch in the Salta mountains of northern Argentina. After Masetti's death, Colomé returned to Cuba. Eleven years later, he went to Angola as chief of the Cuban military mission there.

In another interview, brigadier general Harry Villegas Tamayo, also known by his nom de guerre Pombo, talks about what he calls the most important period of his life: the ten years he fought alongside Che Guevara—from the Sierra Maestra to the internationalist missions in the Congo and Bolivia.

Villegas went to the Congo (now Zaire) in 1965.

"We stayed on Congolese territory for several months," Villegas says, "but because of the position taken by the Organization of African States—that aid could only be provided to the movements fighting against colonialism—we had to leave.

"Che insisted that the request to withdraw our forces be put in writing, so that history could record with absolute clarity Cuba's position in giving internationalist aid to the Congolese people."

In Bolivia, Guevara headed a guerrilla front that set out to build a revolutionary movement of workers and peasants capable of taking power and leading toward socialist revolutions in South America. Che was captured on Oct. 8, 1967, and killed in cold blood the next day by Bolivian army officers after consultation with Washington.

After Che's death, Pombo commanded the six combatants who fought their way out of the encirclement by the U.S.-aided Bolivian armed forces. He tells the story of the Bolivia campaign in detail in the book *Pombo: A Man of Che's Guerrilla*, the English-language edition of which will be released next month by Pathfinder Press.

Many of the generals describe internationalist missions about which little or nothing has been said in writing before.

In Syria and Nicaragua

Néstor López Cuba, for example, describes the mission Cuban internationalists were part of in Syria between 1973 and 1975. In October 1973 the Syrian and Egyptian governments fought a brief war against Israel in an effort to retake sovereign territory occupied by Tel Aviv in 1967 as part of the Zionist regime's decades-long effort to bolster its dispossession of the Palestinian people.

In Syria General López Cuba headed a tank battalion that later grew to a regiment. While the Cubans did not participate directly in combat to take back the Golan Heights, he says, "We maintained a unit in the front for a year. It was a tank squadron. There was some exchange of artillery fire. They damaged two of our tanks. We lived in a hole, in a *chabola*, in conditions of a military campaign. In February 1975 we returned to Cuba. They had promoted me to commander." Ten months later he left for Angola.

López Cuba was also chief of the Cuban military mission in Nicaragua. "It was the most complex, difficult, dangerous, and risky task I ever had," he says.

After the July 1979 revolution in that country that overthrew the U.S.-backed dictatorship of Anastasio Somoza, Washington organized and financed a counterrevolutionary army, known as the contras, which fought against the government of the Sandinista National Liberation Front. The contras were defeated militarily by 1987.

"It was an irregular war, you never knew precisely where the enemy was," López Cuba says. "We had centers of instruction spread throughout the war zone, and our policy was to visit and support these people constantly.

"We traveled in three or four vehicles through routes where we faced ambushes, mine fields. Sometimes we flew in helicopters at low altitudes, just above the tree tops, or between enormous mountains in a little AN-2 plane. On one occasion they hit one of our escort helicopters. We played with our lives every day."

Advising the Nicaraguan army, "was another complex task with great political content," López Cuba tells Báez. "It's much easier to fight than advise."

The Cubans themselves had gone "through the experience of the Soviet advisors. We couldn't impose our criteria. We had to be very careful and consistent. . . . I can say with no doubt that, during the three years and three months I spent in Nicaragua, I carried out the most politically complex mission, and militarily the most difficult and risky task, I ever had."

Many of the generals talk about their experiences in Angola.

"In Angola we gave substantial support to the struggle against apartheid and the battle for the liberation of Namibia," says Ulises del Toro. "The blood spilled shaped forever the identification of the Cuban revolution with the African peoples, an unblemished feat that will one day be recorded in history for what it was."

Hundreds of thousands of Cubans served on internationalist missions in that country from the mid-1970s to the late 1980s. Cuban volunteer troops helped defeat successive invasions of Angola by South Africa's apartheid regime, which joined with U.S.-organized counterrevolutionary efforts to block the Angolan people from realizing their hard-fought independence from Portugal.

The apartheid army was dealt a decisive military defeat at Cuito Cuanavale in March 1988 by the combined forces of the Cuban volunteers, the Angolan army, and fighters from SWAPO (South West Africa People's Organisation).

The victory at Cuito Cuanavale paved the way for the independence of neighboring Namibia. By puncturing once and for all the myth of the white supremacists' invincibility, it gave another impulse to the battle to bring down the apartheid regime itself, which the South African people succeeded in doing half a decade later.

An 'uncontrollable' army

Division general Leopoldo Cintra Frias spent a total of nine years in Angola between 1975 and 1989. Asked about the preparedness of the South African army, he responds, "There are three uncontrollable armies: the South Africans, the Israelis, and the Cubans. The three have different ideologies. The Soviets were never able to control us, even though they tried to on more than one occasion."

"The war in Angola strengthened us politically and ideologically," Cintra Frias says. "It has proved decisive for what we have been able to accomplish during the special period."

Special period is the term Cubans use to describe the extremely difficult economic conditions they have faced since aid and favorable trade relations with the Soviet bloc countries ended abruptly at the beginning of the 1990s and the U.S. economic embargo has been tightened.

"Three hundred thousand Cubans passed through those lands [Angola]. The experience revitalized us, just like in 1959."

PART II

'I SEE CHE AND HIS MEN AS REINFORCEMENTS, AS A DETACHMENT OF INVINCIBLE COMBATANTS'

by Fidel Castro

The following speech was given by Cuban president Fidel Castro in the city of Santa Clara, Villa Clara province, Oct. 17, 1997. Castro was addressing the main ceremony marking the 30th anniversary of the death in combat of Che Guevara, during which the remains of Guevara and six other combatants from Bolivia, Cuba, and Peru who were part of Che's guerrilla in Bolivia were interred. The speech was published in the October 18 issue of the Cuban daily *Granma*. Translation, subheadings, and footnotes are by the *Militant*.

Relatives of the comrades who died in battle; invited guests; residents of Villa Clara; compatriots: [*Applause*]

With deep emotion, we are living through one of those moments that is not often repeated.

We did not come to bid farewell to Che and his heroic comrades. We came to greet them.

I view Che and his men as reinforcements, as a detachment of invincible combatants that this time includes not just Cubans. It also includes Latin Americans who have come to fight at our side and to write new pages of history and glory.

GRANMA/ARNALDO SANTOS

"We did not come here to bid farewell to Che and his heroic comrades," Castro told crowds in Santa Clara. "We came to greet them."

I view Che, furthermore, as a moral giant who grows day by day, whose image, whose strength, whose influence has multiplied throughout the world.

How could he fit below a tombstone?

How could he fit in this plaza?

How could he fit solely in our beloved but small island?

Only the world he dreamed of, which he lived and fought for, is big enough for him.

The more that injustice, exploitation, inequality, unemployment, poverty, hunger, and misery prevail in human society, the more Che's stature will grow.

The more that the power of imperialism, hegemonism, domination, and interventionism grow, to the detriment of the most sacred rights of the peoples—especially the weak, backward, and poor peoples who for centuries were colonies of the West and sources of slave labor—the more the values Che defended will be upheld.

The more that abuses, selfishness, and alienation exist; the more that Indians, ethnic minorities, women, and immigrants suffer discrimination; the more that children are objects of sexual trade or forced into the work force in their hundreds of millions; the more that ignorance, unsanitary conditions, insecurity, and homelessness prevail—the more Che's deeply humanistic message will stand out.

The more that corrupt, demagogic, and hypocritical politicians exist anywhere, the more Che's

Reprinted from *Militant* vol. 61, no. 39, Nov. 10, 1997.

example of a pure, revolutionary, and consistent human being will come through.

The more cowards, opportunists, and traitors there are on the face of the earth, the more Che's personal courage and revolutionary integrity will be admired. The more that others lack the ability to fulfill their duty, the more Che's iron willpower will be admired. The more that some individuals lack the most basic self-respect, the more Che's sense of honor and dignity will be admired. The more that skeptics abound, the more Che's faith in man will be admired. The more pessimists there are, the more Che's optimism will be admired. The more vacillators there are, the more Che's audacity will be admired. The more that loafers squander the product of the labor of others, the more Che's austerity, his spirit of study and work, will be admired.

Forger of others like himself

Che was a true communist and today he is an example and a model of what a revolutionary is and what a communist is.

Che was a teacher and forger of human beings like himself. Consistent in his actions, he always did what he preached, and he always demanded more of himself than of others.

Whenever a volunteer was needed for a difficult mission, he would be the first to step forward, both in wartime and in peacetime. He always subordinated his great dreams to his readiness to generously give his life. Nothing was impossible for him, and he was capable of making the impossible possible.

Among other actions, the invasion from the Sierra Maestra westward through immense and unprotected plains, and the capture of the city of Santa Clara with just a few men, testify to the feats he was capable of.[1]

His ideas concerning revolution in his country of origin and the rest of South America, despite enormous difficulties, were possible. Had they been achieved, perhaps the world today would be different. Vietnam proved that it was possible to fight the interventionist forces of imperialism and defeat them. The Sandinistas [in Nicaragua] defeated one of the most powerful puppets of the United States. The Salvadoran revolutionaries were on the verge of attaining victory. In Africa, apartheid was defeated despite the nuclear weapons it possessed. China, thanks to the heroic struggle of its workers and peasants, is one of the countries with the greatest prospects in the world. Hong Kong had to be returned after 150 years of occupation, which was originally carried out to impose the drug trade on an immense country.

A combatant may die, but not his ideas

Every epoch and every circumstance do not require identical methods and identical tactics. But nothing can stop the course of history; its objective laws have enduring value. Che based himself on those laws and had absolute faith in human beings. Often humanity's great revolutionaries, those responsible for great transformations, did not have the privilege of seeing their dreams realized as quickly as they hoped or desired, but sooner or later they have triumphed.

A combatant may die, but not his ideas.

What was an agent of the U.S. government doing there, where Che was wounded and held captive? Why did they believe that by killing him he would cease to exist as a combatant? Today he is not in La Higuera.[2] Instead, he is everywhere; he is to be found wherever there is a just cause to defend. Those with a stake in eliminating him and making him disappear were incapable of understanding that he had already left an indelible mark on history; that his shining, prophetic vision would become a symbol for all the poor of this world, in their millions. Young people, children, the elderly, men and women who knew him, honest persons throughout the world, regardless of their social origin, admire him.

Che is waging and winning more battles than ever.

Thank you Che, for your personal history, your life, and your example.

Thank you for coming to reinforce us in this difficult struggle we are waging today to save the ideas you fought so hard for, to save the revolution, the homeland, and the conquests of socialism, which is a realization of part of the great dreams you held so dear! [*Applause*] We are counting on you to help us carry out this enormous feat, to defeat the imperialist plans against Cuba, to resist the blockade, to achieve victory. [*Applause*]

As you can see, this land, which is your land; this people, which is your people; this revolution, which is your revolution, continues upholding with honor and pride the banners of socialism. [*Applause*]

Welcome, heroic comrades from the reinforcement detachment. The enemy will never be able to conquer the fortress of ideas and the fortress of justice that you will be defending alongside our people! And together we will continue fighting for a better world!

Hasta la victoria siempre! [Ever onward to victory]

[*Ovation*]

---

1. Guevara commanded the forces that liberated Santa Clara on Jan. 1, 1959, in the last major battle of the revolutionary war that brought down the U.S.-backed Batista dictatorship.

2. La Higuera is the town where Guevara was executed by the Bolivian army.

'CHE CONTINUES TO INSTILL FEAR IN THE OPPRESSORS'

by Ricardo Alarcón

The following speech was given at the opening of an October 1–4 symposium on "Che: Man of the Twenty-First Century," held at the University of Havana and sponsored by the university's Ernesto Guevara Studies Progam along with the Personal Archive of Che Guevara, directed by Aleida March Guevara. Ricardo Alarcón is the president of Cuba's National Assembly and a member of the Political Bureau of the Communist Party of Cuba. Reprinted by permission. The translation, subheadings, and footnotes are by the *Militant*.

Che continues to fight. He represents a real threat that instills fear in the oppressors. This is demonstrated by the abundant literature attempting to distort his life, falsify his thought, and blunt the sharp edge of his image.

A recently published book shows in detail how the CIA, FBI, and other imperialist agencies followed Che's tracks step by step, even before the landing of the *Granma*,[1] and how, through a press that pretends to be free, they strove to distort his efforts. Further documents will be published some day, showing how the imperialists have continued to pursue him systematically from the time of La Higuera[2] to today, as they will surely keep doing in the future.

In the book I alluded to, U.S. attorney Michael Ratner reveals a fact that confirms that Che truly lives—not only in the hearts of youth and the fists of the exploited. In 1988 the region of Bolivia where he fought was still considered a security zone by the authorities. More than 20 years later, a new generation of military officers still seemed to be on the lookout for guerrilla movements around the Ñacahuazú river!

COUNCIL OF STATE OFFICE OF HISTORICAL AFFAIRS

Guevara (with beret) participates in volunteer work in Cuba in early years of revolution. "When some people are giving in or vacillating, we must reproduce Che's unblemished example in the conduct of the vanguard and extend it throughout society. We must cultivate solidarity as a norm of everyday life," Alarcón said.

How should we look at Che today? What is his legacy for the century now beginning? This is the question asked by revolutionaries, those of us who are fighting to transform the world and who believe in the betterment of humanity.

As we do so, his image and his memory spread through the world. His portrait appears on T-shirts worn by youth who never knew him; it is carried during protests by the dispossessed masses who were not able to read his basic writings. It becomes increasingly a symbol that encourages rebellion

Reprinted from *Militant* vol. 61, no. 36, Oct. 20, 1997.

and hope, attaining legendary dimensions.

Conferences like this one can contribute to the collective search needed to begin to find the indispensable answers, which above all must be turned into concrete actions. It could not be otherwise, since the subject of our attention is Ernesto Guevara.

Found time to write about revolution

Besides his enormous contributions as a guerrilla combatant and leader, as well as the important responsibilities he shouldered in the revolutionary government, Che left us a body of writings of astonishing breadth and depth, especially considering they were produced over the course of just a few years by a young leader thoroughly immersed in the storm of events during the most intense period of the life of our people.

In essays, articles, letters, speeches, lectures, and other public addresses, Ernesto Guevara took up the questions that the revolution confronted at that time and made a priceless contribution to the concrete political struggle and revolutionary consciousness of the Cuban people. Imperialism's threats and acts of aggression in that period were subjected to his incisive analysis and his clarifying indictment.

Alert to dangers from the outside, he also focused on questions specifically related to the economy, the trade unions, the formation of the party and its methods and style of work, and the special role played by the youth organizations, among other important subjects. For workers, students, and youth, for political and administrative cadres, he left a wealth of ideas that—aside from conjunctural aspects, of course—remains completely relevant today.

It is remarkable to discover that in the heat of those years, he found time to write about his guerrilla experience in Cuba, leaving subsequent generations a precious testimony that enriches our historic memory. But what surprises others was, for him, something natural and necessary.

Preserving these experiences was essential to the goal—which he carried out with rigorous dedication—of summarizing the story of the Cuban insurrection and elaborating his theory on guerrilla warfare. There, in the concrete development of the armed struggle, where everything depended on each individual combatant, and on their willingness to give their life, he discovered the seeds of the new man.

His intellectual work had an internationalist character that, from the very first article, anticipated his future actions in the Congo and Bolivia. In various international forums he exposed imperialism's criminal exploitation and presented a coherent theory for the liberation of the Third World, without omitting a justified socialist criticism of those who did not practice solidarity as an obligation.

Uncovered roots of events in E. Europe

It is in his study of the questions related to building socialism, registered in his memorable polemics and other basic works, that his thought achieves its greatest depth and begins to anticipate the future. Who could imagine in the early 1960s that a brutal capitalism would reemerge out of European socialism? Who was capable of uncovering the root of the problem and explain it with honesty and courage?

In the battles that imperialism continues to wage against Che we find the greatest proof that he remains alive, that his message prevails. There are attempts to present Ernesto Guevara as a symbol of a bygone era, as something from the past. In the euphoria following the crumbling of the Soviet Union, the imperialist academic establishment—which has joined with others, since cloning existed in the ideological sphere well before it was discovered in the laboratories—has tried to make people believe that the defeat of that model meant the death of the socialist ideal and that this would forever put an end to the movement by workers to achieve that goal.

Che would undoubtedly share our bitterness at the serious setback these events have meant for the people who today are suffering in flesh and blood the experience of real capitalism, and he would understand its negative consequences for the Cuban revolution and for the liberation of the Third World.

His pain would be even greater, similar to that of the wise man who foresaw the inevitable, to that of the messiah who announced the catastrophe and illuminated the road that could have avoided it. He had already warned about how difficult it would be "to defeat capitalism with its own fetishes," and raised this crucial point: "Socialism cannot exist if there is not a change in consciousness that creates a new, fraternal attitude toward humanity, both individually in a society where socialism is being built or has been built, as well as internationally, toward all peoples who suffer imperialist oppression."

His distress would be even deeper and more genuine because, having clarified this question theoretically, he preached by example both "in the society in which socialism is being built"—through his austerity; his total devotion to revolutionary activity; his genuine, modest, and quiet participation in voluntary labor—as well as in his attitude "toward all peoples oppressed by imperialism," as he would demonstrate more eloquently a few months later.

But before resuming the guerrilla path, he explained, in one of his most widely circulated works, his concern about the challenges facing a nascent socialist society: "There is the danger that the forest will not be seen for the trees. The pipe dream that socialism can be achieved with the help of the dull instruments left to us by capitalism (the commodity as the economic cell, profitability, individual material interest as a lever, etc.) can lead into a blind alley. And you wind up there after having traveled a long distance with many crossroads, and it is hard to figure out just where you took the wrong turn. Meanwhile, the economic foundation that has been laid has done its work of undermining the development of consciousness. To build communism it is necessary, simultaneous with the new material foundations, to build the new man."[3]

His creative and truly Marxist thought allowed him to foresee the fate of that experience and discover the roots of its failure at a time when the very theoreticians of anticommunism considered it unchangeable and when the predominant dogmatism within the left clouded judgments. The new man was certainly not the one who had been defeated, but rather "the pipe dream of achieving socialism" without him.

Nor did capitalism achieve a global victory over the forces of socialism and national liberation. It did achieve a temporary victory through the lack of consistent and united action by these forces, which were unable to take advantage of a favorable international balance of forces. In short, what was missing was the duplication of Che's heroic example and the application of his ideas by the revolutionary movement as a whole.

Events vindicate Che

The dramatic events of recent years are not a defeat for Che but are rather his vindication. That is why Che lives, why he is taking on gigantic proportions, springing up everywhere, and advancing. That is why his enemies' fears grow.

His humanistic, renovational, and ethical conception of socialism enriched the Cuban revolutionary process and has been present throughout its history, in competition, of course, with tropical expressions of "real socialism" and in the midst of the most far-reaching confrontation ever with imperialism. Even when erroneous views and negative tendencies predominated in the leadership and administration of the economy, Che's legacy survived among us by remaining intact in foreign policy, reaching extraordinary levels that propagated his example on a massive scale.

The process of rectification of errors and negative tendencies, initiated by Fidel Castro in 1986, revived the revolutionary spirit and confirmed the correctness of Ernesto Guevara's ideas and teachings.

Before real socialism's course toward bankruptcy had become visible, Cuban revolutionaries, inspired by Che, were deepening the struggle against its causes and attacking the root of the problem.

The authentic character of the Cuban revolution, which was exclusively the product of our own history, the result of the struggles and sacrifices of Cubans; its genuinely independent character; and the intelligent, consistent, and firm hand of its central leader, explain why those pernicious elements did not acquire the uncontrollable dimensions that led to the disintegration of the European experience.

The Cuban revolution did not succumb as the empire's chiefs and pimps had predicted a few years ago. It was able to resist the terrible consequences of the sudden disappearance of its markets, the complete loss of foreign credit and financing, the drastic reduction of supplies of oil and raw materials and other vital imports. It was able to do so and even begin to recover economically despite the fact that Washington's economic war against us came on top of the blow suffered by the disintegration of the USSR.

What does Che mean today for Cuba and the Cuban people? How should we integrate him into the current situation, into our perspectives and aspirations? What is his role, as a son of our people and one of its most clear-sighted leaders, in the complex, difficult, and decisive stage we are now going through? What should we do about his revolutionary passion, his unflagging militancy, his creative thinking?

Let us state the obvious. He is with us here and now, fighting stubbornly to rescue his work and his dreams as a builder.

Need Che's ideas today

Under the particular circumstances of this period—when in order to save our socialism, the only socialism possible in Cuba today, we have been forced to make concessions, we have had to introduce into our society undesirable values that are alien to his values—we need Che more than ever. Because of the fact that the inevitable changes in our society and the brutal imperialist offensive introduce new—and sometimes more subtle and serpentine—elements in the ideological struggle, Che is indispensable for us. We must take his ideas and turn them into a vital guide for workers, students, professors, and the entire people. At a time when the poison of selfish individualism threatens us from the inside, when some people are giving in or vacillating, we must reproduce his unblemished example in the conduct of the vanguard and extend it throughout society.

We must cultivate solidarity as a norm of everyday life.

Through the systematic involvement of the workforce and its unions, it is necessary to make the utmost efforts toward economic recovery, to save our resources, raise productivity and efficiency, especially in the state sector, combat indiscipline, and strengthen the cohesion and unity of all revolutionaries and patriots.

We must strengthen the role of the party, perfect our democratic system and the work of the mass organizations and our socialist civil society as a whole, and develop consistently popular participation in and controls over these bodies. What the invincible guerrilla is calling for is more socialism on the political-ideological level, a more heroic, creative, and Cuban socialism.

We will be like Che, our children declare. This is not just a beautiful phrase. It captures a strategy and a hope. The homeland will be saved; the revolution will prevail; our socialism will survive and be better and more genuine if we are capable, as a people, of being like him, of fighting and living like him.

Thirty-five years ago, during "the brilliant yet sad days" of the October crisis,[4] when the threat of total extermination hung over Cuba, Ernesto Guevara left us this message, which remains true for today and all time:

"From here, from their solitary vanguard trench, our people are making their voices heard. It is not the swan song of a defeated revolution, but a revolutionary hymn that is destined to become eternal on the lips of fighters throughout the Americas. It resonates with history."

From here, from his indestructible trench, let us tell him once again:

¡Hasta la victoria siempre! [Forward ever to victory]

¡Socialismo o muerte! [Socialism or death]

¡Patria o muerte! [Homeland or death]

---

1. In late 1956, Fidel Castro, Che Guevara, and 80 other members of the July 26 Movement left Mexico and arrived in Cuba aboard the yacht *Granma* to initiate the revolutionary war against the Batista dictatorship.

2. La Higuera is the Bolivian village where Guevara was killed.

3. See Guevara, *Socialism and Man in Cuba*, published by Pathfinder Press.

4. Amid escalating preparations by Washington for a new invasion of Cuba in the spring and summer of 1962, the Cuban government signed a mutual defense agreement with the Soviet Union. In October 1962 President John Kennedy demanded removal of Soviet nuclear missiles installed in Cuba following the signing of that pact. Washington ordered a naval blockade of Cuba, stepped up its preparations to invade, and placed U.S. armed forces on nuclear alert. Cuban workers and farmers mobilized in the millions to defend the revolution. Following an exchange of communications between Washington and Moscow, Soviet premier Nikita Khrushchev, without consulting the Cuban government, announced his decision to remove the missiles on October 28.

CENTRAL GOAL OF SOCIALISM IS THE CREATION OF NEW MAN

Interview with Orlando Borrego

by Ariel Terrero

The following interview with Orlando Borrego appeared in issue no. 10, 1997, of the international edition of the Cuban magazine *Bohemia*, under the title "Dream and Prophecy." Borrego worked closely with Ernesto Che Guevara in Cuba's Ministry of Industry, which Guevara headed in the early 1960s, and is a former Minister of Sugar. Reprinted by permission. The translation and footnotes are by the *Militant*.

Although he has obtained a doctorate in economics, Orlando Borrego will always be, in spirit, the grumpy accountant who Ernesto Che Guevara once asked to work with him. Before giving a green light to the interview, he rapidly scans the questions, with avowed distrust and a careful eye. Fortunately, he eventually bestows his trust and speaks freely.

He was 21 years old when Che put him at the head of the Military Economic Junta of the La Cabaña fortress, after this Havana outpost fell into the hands of the Rebel Army. Later he was one of the first men who the mythic Argentine took with him to the Department of Industrialization of the Agrarian Reform Institute. He spent six years very close to Che, starting from when he joined Che's guerrilla column in the Escambray in 1958.

PRENSA LATINA

MILITANT/MARTIN KOPPEL

Above, Guevara visits a factory in the province of Pinar del Río, 1962. From left to right: a local party leader, Che Guevara, army captain Pablo Rivalta, Orlando Borrego, and Aleida March, Guevara's wife. "There was nothing utopian in Che," said Borrego, **right.**

"I always say these were the equivalent of 10 or 12 years, because this was very intense, hard work, with days extending to two or three in the morning," says the present consultant to the Ministry of Transportation and the hotel chain Horizontes.

Later he was first vice-chairman and then minister of the sugar industry. But even in this last stage he continued working under Che. "He was my boss; I consulted with him about everything." And I suspect he has never stopped doing it.

From such a close relationship, Borrego retains experiences, very personal memories, and documents, some unpublished, in which, for example,

Reprinted from *Militant* vol. 61, no. 37, Oct. 27, 1997.

Che anticipated the debacle European socialism would undergo 25 years later.

QUESTION: In your opinion, what characteristics of Che's were most in harmony with his work as minister of industry?

ANSWER: Che lacked experience as a statesman in that period, but he had various things in his favor. He was a man endowed with a very developed intelligence, and an extremely broad education. He was also aided by his inclination toward industrial activity. In the Sierra Maestra, as soon as he received the command of a guerrilla column, he organized a series of production activities: bakeries, shoe factories, weapons repair shops. . . . When he arrived at La Cabaña he did the same.

He also had iron discipline, dedication, exceptional will-power, a very original method of engaging others to participate in work, extraordinary interest in the development of the country, and knowledge acquired in the Sierra Maestra about Cuba, its history, and even its economy.

QUESTION: Che is remembered above all as a guerrilla leader. What in your opinion weighs most in history: Che's military ideas or the economic concepts he developed and applied?

ANSWER: Perhaps the loss of Che is felt more keenly in his capacity as a revolutionary thinker than as a guerrilla. In that period he was making contributions to the ideas of socialism, with extraordinary value for the present and the future. It seems, however, that not many people in the world see things that way. Despite the great influence that Che exercises among the peoples, all of his ideas, as a whole, are still little known. Everyone takes Che in their own manner. Some see him as a guerrilla, others as a legendary figure, others value his capacity for sacrifice, his humanism, or the ethics of his life.

QUESTION: What principles and characteristics of the economy under socialism did Che put the most trust in?

ANSWER: The central point in his vision of a socialist society was the development of the individual, the creation of a new man. That is the essence of everything he sought. Che was opposed to seeing socialist society as simply a question of production to satisfy the material needs of the individual. He used to say that this is what capitalism does, at the cost of exploitation. It is a tendency toward consumerism and nothing more. Che stressed as the central goal of a socialist society the creation of a new man—a man of solidarity, ethics, culture, and with the highest values that a human being could have; a patriot, sensitive toward any human being in the world. He liked to repeat Martí's idea: "Every true man must feel on his own cheek every blow dealt against the cheek of another."

The development of the productive forces under socialism must be indissolubly linked to the formation and training of the human being. Che set no time period to achieve this objective, but he was convinced of it. If these two lines of approach are not developed in a parallel way until they join up together; if emphasis is given to consumerism and material production and the individual is forgotten, then it is possible to attain a very high level of production and a deformed, selfish individual, similar to the one in capitalist societies.

QUESTION: Because of the emphasis he puts on humanism, some theoreticians—including on the left—classify Che's ideas as utopian, and some even say that they were an expression of a petty-bourgeois philosophy. What do you think?

ANSWER: Many people insulted Che, and not only in the capitalist world. In the Soviet Union and other socialist countries they also called him an idealist, revisionist, Proudhonian, etc. In contemporary bourgeois literature the same thing happens, but this literature has a conception of what a successful man is that has nothing to do with Che or Fidel. They are called idealists, romantics; and are given no credit for the influence they have had in the social transformations of the 20th century.

There is no revolutionary without dreams. If there were, he would lack inspiration to fight. But in my judgment, there is nothing idealistic or utopian in Che. I worked with him and saw him develop these ideas not only in a theoretical form, but in practice.

Che's effort to develop consciousness in our country has had tangible results. Many people in other countries ask me whether something of the new man exists in Cuba, and I personally am convinced there is. That is the way we can stand up today. The revolution has withstood the Special

Period[1] and all that came with the collapse of the socialist camp, together with the blockade, because there is a consciousness and a people that have known how to uphold revolutionary ideas, and meet the challenges required by the historic moment. And among the Cuban people, the attitude of our young people has extraordinary weight. They are an essential pillar of the revolution.

QUESTION: Nevertheless, man under socialism has not developed a consciousness as owner of the means of production, something fundamental to this system. There has even been talk of a certain alienation of the worker toward his condition as owner, and that property is state-owned, and not social.

ANSWER: That is an old polemic, one that concerns a crucial aspect of socialism. But I would not speak of alienation. Che did not set time limits for the development of consciousness in socialism. For him it was a long process in which there could be advances and retreats. I am reminded of him very much with the Special Period. People who advanced in the development of consciousness have flagged in the face of shortages, they have retreated, and some have even betrayed. Fortunately, they have been a minority.

The question of acquiring real consciousness of social property—and above all that this property be highly productive and efficient—is a very complex one. We should keep working at it, above all, at putting it into practice.

In addition to applying intelligent methods to educate the individual, a great deal needs to be done in the field of management techniques and incentives. Che never rejected material incentives, but he emphasized moral ones, so the individual would increasingly acquire more consciousness of social property to make it more effective. Eventually the moment will be reached when the individual produces out of his social duty toward work.

QUESTION: Was Che's departure for the Congo and later Bolivia an expression of confidence in the fate of the Cuban revolution? Do you believe he would have taken another decision if he knew what Cuba would confront in the 1990s?

ANSWER: In my opinion he would not have changed his decision. As Fidel has explained, from the time he was in Mexico, Che had expected to continue the struggle in Latin America, and specifically in Argentina, after the Cuban revolution triumphed. But I also think he departed confident that the revolution was in an advanced process of consolidation. I can state with certainty that Che was confident that if Cuba applied its own viewpoint and had a leader such as Fidel, there was no cause for concern about the stability and leadership of our revolution.

QUESTION: Did he have confidence, then, that socialism was irreversible?

ANSWER: In the case of Cuba, yes.

QUESTION: But did he believe in the irreversibility of socialism in general? In other words, would Che have been surprised by the fall of the Berlin Wall?

ANSWER: He believed that society on a world scale would go forward toward socialism. For him this was the solution to the problems of humanity. Nevertheless, Che did not believe that the socialist model of the Soviet Union and the other countries of Eastern Europe was viable or correct. After he became familiar with the conceptions of how the economy was being directed in these countries, he expressed great reservations, and predicted, 25 years in advance, that this model was heading back toward capitalism.

QUESTION: Reservations about which tendencies?

ANSWER: He did not accept the view developed with the New Economic Policy in the Soviet Union.[2] Che felt that Lenin was forced to make concessions and apply the NEP owing to the complex and difficult political and economic situation of the country at that time. But Lenin died almost immediately, and his successors did not make a correction in time. Che felt that introducing capitalist categories in socialist countries threw them off course, with all the consequences this brought for the formation of the new man and for society as a whole, including its effects on the system's superstructure. They did not promote the search for economic mechanisms appropriate to socialism, and arrived at a dead end, which would produce a return to capitalism. That was Che's assessment.

QUESTION: Where did he say this?

ANSWER: In a still-unpublished manuscript he sent me attached to a letter, at the end of 1965, after the campaign in the Congo ended. In that analysis Che stated the following:

"The changes produced by the New Economic Policy, the NEP, have penetrated so deeply into the life of the Soviet Union that they have left their mark on this entire stage, and the results are discouraging. The capitalist superstructure has influenced, in a sharper and sharper way, the relations of production, and the conflicts provoked by the hybrid that the NEP was, are being resolved today in favor of the superstructure. There is a regression toward capitalism."

QUESTION: Even so, other experiences accept a larger role for the market in the socialist economy. How would Che view what is happening in Cuba, for example?

ANSWER: The current moment is very different from the one we are analyzing in relation to the polemic on models of economic management in socialism. How do I picture Che? I picture him studying and obtaining a deeper theoretical understanding, doing a careful analysis of the phenomenon of globalization and all these backward ideas of neoliberalism. I picture him trying to give a practical solution to the extraordinary shortages and difficulties we have in Cuba, while avoiding concessions of principle in the management of the economy that could bring disastrous consequences to our revolutionary process, as happened in the former Soviet Union.

There are concepts in Che's body of ideas that can and must be applied at the present time, and others that should be adapted to current conditions, which are very different than those existing then. And I believe Fidel is doing this: making indispensable changes to survive, because it would be absurd not to make them, but with no concessions of principle that would lead us toward reversing the progress we've obtained and the values we've achieved in developing a higher form of society.

QUESTION: In light of everything that has happened in recent years, does history have any debt to Che?

ANSWER: If not a debt, then a certain commitment, a commitment that implies concrete actions by all sensible and honest persons in the world to appropriate the most valuable parts of his historical legacy. In turning himself into a model of the new man owing to his ideas and exceptional qualities, Che represented an essential point in the progress of humanity, in the search for a higher form of life for human beings.

QUESTION: And does Che have any debt to history?

ANSWER: Che would have to respond to this. But if I am asked, I believe that Che was a man who was never satisfied, who always considered his contributions to be small. His plans and ideas were so ambitious and creative that I imagine he would feel a debt to history. Perhaps what would pain him most would be to not have continued in other countries the job he began in Cuba and left as an extraordinary heritage. He would feel it his debt, perhaps, not having seen the development of a new man on a broader scale, on a world scale, or at least, in Latin America. That was his dream.

---

1. "Special Period" is the term used in Cuba to describe the economic crisis triggered by the collapse in long-standing trade relations with the Soviet Union and Eastern European countries at the start of the 1990s.

2. The New Economic Policy was adopted by the Russian Communist Party in March 1921, following the economic devastation caused by World War I and the subsequent civil war. Aimed at reviving an economy in which industrial production had fallen to less than 20 percent of prewar levels, the measure allowed a limited return to free trade and the operation of foreign concessions alongside the nationalized sectors of the economy.

GUEVARA: 'HUMAN BEINGS ARE NO LONGER BEASTS OF BURDEN'

by Enrique Oltuski

The following is a speech given by Enrique Oltuski at a conference at the University of Havana on "Che: Man of the Twenty-First Century," October 1–4. Oltuski worked closely with Ernesto Che Guevara in the Ministry of Industry, which Guevara headed in the early 1960s, and today is Cuba's deputy minister of fishing. Reprinted by permission. Translation, subheadings, and footnotes are by the *Militant*.

What is happening in the world that makes the figure of Che grow larger and larger every day. Is it not because he fills a moral void? Is it not because he inspires confidence in the future? Is it not because he is the human being we all want to be? Is it not because Che is the herald of the new man?

GRANMA

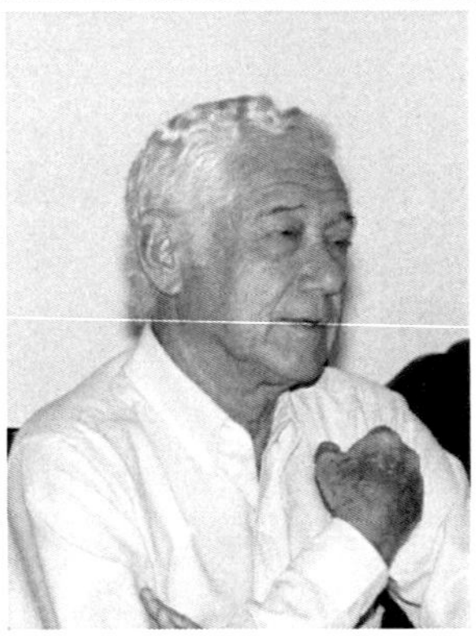

MILITANT/MARTIN KOPPEL

Above, Che Guevara taking over as president of Cuba's National Bank, November 1959. From left, José Naranjo, Osmany Cienfuegos, Osvaldo Dorticós, Che Guevara, (unknown), Felipe Pazos, Enrique Oltulski, Faustino Pérez. **Right,** Oltulski speaking in a conference "The 21st Century: the Legacy and Relevancy of Che's Works," held in Havana, September 25–27, sponsored by *Tricontinental* magazine.

Asthma, which he eventually would bring under control with his willpower and which he began to suffer at age two, compelled him to rest during periods of acute attacks. As a child of educated parents, books were familiar objects in the house, and thus books became a refuge over long hours.

As a 15-year-old he read Freud, Verlaine, Mallarmé, Zola, Sarmientos, Faulkner, Steinbeck. An interesting mix of authors, seeds of the future forest of ideas, planted as yet with no order.

Over time and as his intellect grew, his interest in works with a social content grew. He intensified his reading of Marxism and also read Kafka, Camus, and Sartre.

His travels to South America were decisive in his formation. He became conscious of the Indian of the Americas; there arose in him a fraternal spirit toward the indigenous peoples. With his stay in the mines of Chuquicamata in Chile, he got to know

Reprinted from *Militant* vol. 61, no. 38, Nov. 3, 1997.

the life of the copper miners, and the oppression they are subjected to by the Yankee owners. He felt in his own blood and bone how the U.S. archeologists pillaged the ruins of Machu Picchu. His love for his fellow man led him to live side by side with lepers, who bid him farewell as a brother.

He met Bolivian and Guatemalan revolutionaries. In Mexico he joined up with the Cuban revolution. He was no longer a mere spectator; he was now a revolutionary who wanted to change things.

When they went to the encampments in the final stage of their training as a *Granma*[1] expeditionary, Che told of his travels through Latin America. The anecdotal side was not what he wanted to stress; rather the poverty, how the people lived, how the Mayan Indians lived in Guatemala, the corruption of the governments. He wrote a great deal on these topics: his trip from one country to the other, the persons he met, but above all the poverty, the state of slavery that the Indian of the Americas lived in.

Later came the epic events in Cuba, his apprenticeship as a guerrilla together with his teacher Fidel; the invasion, the battle of Santa Clara, the Ministry of Industry.

With the Ministry of Industry the first steps were taken to create an organizational structure of a socialist character in Cuba. The system of management being developed at the time was based on a fundamental theoretical conception; the aim was to develop man's consciousness and to develop the productive forces in such a way that, in a given period of time, the development of the productive forces would coincide with the formation of the new man. In this way a just society would be created, where man would be brother of man, and where happiness of the individual would be the happiness of all.

The system of the Ministry of Industry was being consolidated as the result of an experience where man was at the center. Man's education, the development of his consciousness, and moral and material incentives played a principal role.

The element of voluntary work

A new element made its appearance as part of this conception: voluntary work. Che characterized voluntary work as an absolutely selfless contribution, a transformation of work into a social duty—and more than a duty, a social pleasure. The idea of work as a completely integral function of man was also part of the theoretical conception that Che was completing during his years in Cuba.

In August 1964, at a ceremony awarding communist certificates to the best workers of the Ministry of Industry, Che, with his fine human sensibility, cited a few paragraphs from a book by the poet León Felipe:

"But man is a hard-working and stupid child, who has turned work into tiresome toil, he has turned the drumstick into a hoe, and instead of tapping out a song of joy on the land, he began to dig. . . ."

The poet continued:

"I want to say that no one has been able to dig to the rhythm of the sun, and that no one has yet cut a stalk of corn with love and grace."

Che stated in reply:

"That's why I wanted to quote those lines. Because today we could tell that great desperate poet to come to Cuba to see how man, after passing through all the stages of capitalist alienation, and after being considered a beast of burden harnessed to the yoke of the exploiter, has rediscovered his course, has found his way back. Today in our Cuba, work takes on new meaning every day. It is done with new joy."

And we say as in the song: Che, you are the poet.

But there was another element in the conception of the new life, the new society, the new man. It was the human warmth that consciousness also develops. This too was part of forming the new man.

But . . . what was Che's personal life like? How was this human sensibility manifested, a sensibility that has so rarely been reached? Let us poke through the recollections of those who had the privilege of knowing him.

Stories of those who worked with Che

Arsacio Vanegas, the Mexican who trained the future guerrillas in the Sierra Maestra, relates the following:

"I opened the door that afternoon in Mexico City, as I was attending to my friend María Antonia González, who was then ill, and whose house served as general headquarters to the Cuban exiles.

"Before me appeared a young man, with uncombed hair, attractive in appearance, whose clothing indicated that his economic situation was not particularly flourishing.

"'I'm looking for Ñico López,' he said.

"'Who's looking for him?'

"'Doctor Guevara.'

"'I'm sorry, but he's not here.'

"The voice of María Antonia came from inside the apartment.

"'Who is it, Vanegas?'

"'A young doctor who's looking for Ñico.'

"'Well, stop fooling around, tell him to go to hell. This isn't the time for social visits.'

"'It's the owner of the house, María Antonia González, and she doesn't feel well.'" Vanegas said, trying to smooth things over.

"'Boy, does she have a temper,' said the young man. He left a message and rapidly left.

"The day Che and Fidel met they talked a long time. I waited outside and when they left the house where they were meeting, Fidel told me:

"'Vanegas, my friend, Doctor Guevara is now a member of the July 26 Movement. Make arrangements with him to begin his training.'

"I told Che to bring adequate clothing because we would be scaling some hills. We would meet near Guadalupe, at the Buenavista movie theater. Everybody was assembled there and we began to walk north. As we climbed the hill we practiced how to breathe, how to guide ourselves, learning which direction was north, where the sun rose, where it set. Days later we quickened the pace. It was very hard to climb the hill with its steep slopes. Che had gone separately, falling behind, and suddenly I heard a strange sound. I told the guys to keep walking, and I went back to where Che was.

"'What's the matter, doctor?' He didn't say anything to me. He made signs for me to wait, and I did so for a long time, until his attack of asthma passed.

"'I don't want you to tell anybody what happened, Vanegas, because this must not hinder me from going on the expedition.'

"I tried to limit Che in the exercises, because I was concerned with his asthma. Che eventually became very upset, and told me, 'Don't prohibit me from doing exercises. They don't affect me, and if they do, it's my problem.'

"When the exercises began in the gym, I taught the people to defend themselves, how to grab other people's clothes, how to hit someone, what the vulnerable parts are, how to hurt them, even to the point of causing death, and so on. One day he called to me:

"'Hey, Vanegas, how long are we going to go through this routine. What is it we're learning? I'm not going to join the circus or be a gymnast.'

"I said something rude to him, and grabbed him by surprise and threw him on the canvas. 'This is what I'm showing you, and if you don't know how to defend yourself, I'm going to break your arm.'

"He remained there thinking, and said to me with a humility that I found moving:

"'That's OK, Vanegas. You're right. Pardon me.'"

Enemies of Cuba falsify Che's image

Orlando Borrego, Che's first deputy minister of the Ministry of Industry, tells us:

"Today Che is a figure of world stature. Now that Che is an example and a banner of young people around the world, the enemies of the Cuban revolution are trying to give a false image of his personality. Today those of us who had the privilege of knowing him and living at his side during that fleeting but profound stay in our country, cannot fail to remember his affection and human warmth in his relations with his comrades during wartime, with the workers during peacetime, with his subordinates in the Ministry of Industry, with his family, with members of his escort, with his friends, and above all, with Fidel."

Aleida March, his companion in the mountains of the Escambray, in the battle of Santa Clara, and in life, recalls:

"Che spent very little time at home. Only Saturday night and some Sunday afternoons, after voluntary work. There was never a lot of time to talk. Che told me to study history, that someday we would sit down together in front of the fire to talk about this favorite topic of his, and that was what I studied when he went off to Bolivia.

"After the Africa campaign we were together in Tanzania for almost a month and we talked about many things we had not had time to speak about before. We read and Che wrote. In Prague, for the first time, we had a home life. I cooked, washed the clothes. We lived the life we had not been able to.

"At the beginning Che did not want to return. He thought this would implicate Cuba, but Fidel insisted he come and train.

"During the training in Cuba, I brought Celita and Ernestico, the youngest children, to see him. I didn't bring the older ones, so that they wouldn't recognize him. Che wanted to have children. The children were more attached to me, because they saw their father so little. He used to say: 'Enjoy them now because when they're older they'll be mine. Before the birth of Aleidita, our first child, Che thought it would be a boy and wanted to name him Ernesto. I said no, that calling him Ernesto Guevara would be a large burden for him to carry. 'We'll name him Camilo,'[2] Che compromised. 'That way he'll be a combination of two guerrilla fighters.'

"I didn't think Che would one day leave Cuba, until he returned from Africa and told me that this time the departure for Bolivia would be definitive. Che did not think about death; he was always an optimist. He thought he would triumph and that we would be reunited later.

"Che liked poetry. He left behind letters to his children, his parents, and his closest comrades. He left me a tape recording of his voice, with the poems he loved most."

Revolution is more than social justice

Harry Villegas, "Pombo," who was with Che from age 16, tells us:

"With Che we learned what the revolution really was. The revolution was not only a question of social justice, but a moral question. For us it was a new outlook on life; simply put, it was to become a new man. The revolution wasn't a question of living one day at a time; Che set goals for us, objectives for which it was necessary to fight each day. That was what it meant to be a revolutionary.

"My relations with Che began as those between a commander and his subordinate. Che was always our commander, our guide, and as such we respected him. But gradually and in a very subtle way, these relations became transformed into more fraternal ties and sentiments, of comrades, of friends. We saw his concern for us, as if he were our father. He wanted to prepare us for when the revolution triumphed, so we could be useful in building the new society.

"On October 8, 1967, I was 100 meters from Che in the Yuro ravine, although I didn't know this at the time. The ravine was in front of us and further, behind the ravine, was the little schoolhouse at La Higuera. We saw the movement, we heard the soldiers speaking, all of which gives an idea of how close we were.

"The news reached us via the radio. They gave details of how Che was dressed, of his two watches, since he also carried the watch Tuma had left with him before dying, to give to his son. All that convinced us that Che had really been killed.

"For us this was a mortal blow. At first, we felt crestfallen. But we were children of Che. We were the clay he had molded, and we understood that one had to overcome that state of mind, and we were able to overcome it. We reached the conclusion that the war was not over, that Che continued to be present among us with his ideas and his example, that it was necessary to continue the struggle until the final victory, something that revolutionaries could achieve."

Reviewing everything said by Vanegas, Aleida, Borrego, Harry, and many comrades who knew Che, who lived side-by-side with him, who were influenced by his ideas and above all his example, confirms once again his exceptional qualities as a revolutionary, because a revolutionary is one who changes things. His thinking knew no boundaries, and neither did his confidence in man.

The idea that the development of social consciousness would give birth to the new man, where intelligence triumphs over natural forces and where both of these triumph over personal selfishness, is the central concept of his thought and the force that moves and will continue to move men of good will around the world.

All this intellectual and physical strength harbored a sensitive man, human, who loved, laughed, joked, composed and recited verses, and who at the same time would suffer the injustices of the world he wanted to change.

The example, the teachings of Che have not died with him, nor have the men who can carry them out. Because despite having been an exceptional individual, Che was not someone out of reach. As Fidel once said about Camilo, among the peoples of the world there are many Ches, and they will complete his work.

1. *Granma* was the name of the boat that carried 82 revolutionary combatants, including Che and Fidel Castro, from Mexico to Cuba in December 1956. The fighters formed the core of the Rebel Army that led the struggle to overturn the U.S.-backed Batista dictatorship.

2. Camilo Cienfuegos was a *Granma* expeditionary who rose to commander in the Rebel Army in January 1959. He became Rebel Army chief of staff. His plane was lost at sea on October 28, 1959.

'THIS WAS THE WORK OF A GIANT'

Interview with Arturo Guzmán

by Julio García Luís

The interview below is with Arturo Guzmán, who worked in the Ministry of Industry with Che and who is today an economic advisor to CUBALSE, a Cuban state import company. The interview was originally published in the Oct. 6, 1997, issue of *Trabajadores*, the weekly newspaper of the Central Organization of Cuban Workers (CTC), under the title "The work of a giant." Reprinted by permission. Translation and footnotes are by the *Militant*.

Ernesto Che Guevara, left, presenting award for voluntary work in 1964 union meeting. At center is Cuban trade union leader Lázaro Peña.

Guzmán's time is just about freely convertible. His current job as financial adviser to CUBALSE is directly linked to the intense effort to obtain hard currency, and he puts all his long experience in economic management into this task. Additionally, he does not like to squander what for him is "something very intimate, cherished memories." He is referring to the early 1960s, when he held a whole range of management responsibilities in the Ministry of Industry, from factory administrator up to working closely with Che as first deputy minister.

Nevertheless, his kindness, in combination with the spirit of those days of remembrance, proved stronger. In the end, he made time to see us.

"I did not know Che. I had been involved in the clandestine struggle in Havana and was a professional accountant. In February 1960 I received a sheet of paper designating me as administrator of an 'intervened' factory called Técnica Cubana, in Cárdenas. This was a plant producing paper from sugarcane bagasse.

"A short time after that, I saw Che for the first time. He came to visit the factory, and we showed him the installations and explained the production process. Afterward I asked if he wanted to see more. 'Where are the warehouses?' he asked. We went there and he began to examine the packing slips, in order to verify that what each one said matched what was actually there. Aleida, his companion, helped him. She would read: 'x amount of 15-watt light bulbs' and there had to be that number of bulbs. He was giving me a practical lesson that's lasted my entire life. 'This is important,' he was telling me. 'It is your responsibility. Nothing can be missing here.'

"I think that to be able to assess what this extraordinary man did at the National Bank, the

Reprinted from *Militant* vol. 61, no. 40, Nov. 17, 1997.

Department of Industrialization of the National Institute of Agrarian Reform, and the Ministry of Industry," Guzmán states, "one would have to recreate the whole atmosphere of those days, which you would find hard to understand if you didn't live through them.

"The conditions were exceptionally adverse. First of all there was the exodus of technicians. In Técnica Cubana, when I arrived, there were 18 engineers—Cuban, Canadian, and North American. In a short time, there were only two Cuban engineers left, plus one middle-level technician.

"There was no machine tool industry on a national level. The U.S. blockade of spare parts, raw materials, and goods of every type was getting under way, and there were no means to produce spare parts. We didn't even have the blueprints to make them. One must remember that 95 percent of the basic means of production that were nationalized came from the U.S. There was enormous dependency. That is the context in which Che accomplished the feat of avoiding a collapse of industry, maintaining production, organizing it, and even managing to make it grow steadily. Statistics of the time show that between 1960 and 1967 industry grew at an average annual rate of 4 percent.

"What's more, this was done over five years, and with scientific and technical personnel like ourselves, to boot. We were people with no training; combatants of different backgrounds, with no authority other than our political credibility.

"Just so you get an idea, on August 10, 1963, all the administrators of industry in the country took an exam, and it was determined that anyone lacking a sixth-grade education could not continue in administration. There were 132 comrades who had to either go back to school, or return to their original work places. Looking at it from today's standpoint, having a sixth-grade education is nothing great.

"At a meeting shortly after that, Che stated that his Directing Council—that is, all of us—were "makeshift luminaries." And he didn't stop there. He gave us a period of 10 years to obtain a university degree in the fields we were heading. Since I knew this wasn't a joke but was very serious, I went and enrolled in industrial engineering.

"Once he gave us a little book on linear equations. Then, every so often, he would ask me—and I imagine he did this with the others—whether I had read the book, whether I had studied it. Finally he realized that we were not making great use of the book, and he called us together one day at 7:00 in the morning, and began to give us classes."

His vision of the future

"One of the things that should be stressed is the all-embracing nature of the system Che created in the Ministry of Industry. There was a policy on cadre development, an economic policy, a policy on scientific development, there was a plan for future perspectives, we talked about making chemicals from sugarcane in the long term, of the production of nickel, steel, fertilizers. . . .

"The basic feature of the cadre policy was promotion of scientific and technical personnel from the ranks, based on performance on the job. At a certain moment, with one or two exceptions, all of us on the Directing Council came from the ranks.

"In addition, the cadre policy was based on great rigor in selecting scientific and technical personnel, and a demanding attitude toward the fulfillment of tasks. In the ministry there was a system of councils, offices, and meetings. Agreed-to tasks were to be carried out to the letter. If an agreement could not be fulfilled, you were required to submit in writing, prior to the deadline, the reasons for it, and you had to receive written authorization for nonfulfillment of the agreement.

"Fifteen minutes after the time set for a meeting, no latecomers would be allowed in. Discipline was conscious, above all, but it was also obligatory. If you failed to meet an agreed-upon task, you weren't scolded, you were sanctioned. Every day that a statistical report was delayed was one day's less pay for the director responsible. Guanahacabibes was set up to deal with administrative problems of a more serious nature.[1] In other words, 'Praise the lord, but pass the ammunition.'

"Che's emphasis on reducing costs is completely valid today. He promoted the use of statistics and economic projections, economic analysis, mathematical techniques. At that time there was a large computer, an Elliot, which occupied the entire basement of the Ministry of Labor and was run from there. Who knows what Che would have achieved with today's computers?

"I was director of the heavy chemical branch of industry for a time, and discussions on the production plan were held on the sixth or eighth of every month. Those days and no others. Which means that you had to have your report ready. I had a Friden, a gigantic machine, and I was extremely happy that they gave it to me. Now, on the fifth of the month, the country's books were closed for record keeping. And it was record keeping that was 100 percent accurate, because if it wasn't accurate . . . if you came to the Ministry of Industry with a report that had inaccurate figures—well, better you should dry up and disappear before entering. There was one type of record keeping—accurate—and that's that.

"Moreover, one must keep in mind that everything was within a single ministry. For example, when I was leading the heavy chemical branch, there were five enterprises in it, and one of them was the Consolidated Sugar Enterprise headed by Alfredo Menéndez and Esteban Breto, with a team of technical personnel, and it produced six million tons of sugar a year.

"We had a really powerful apparatus of supervision: it eventually had some 400 members, between accountants and inspectors, to review performance of that entire industrial universe.

"It was a systematic, rigorous job that compelled you to respond at every moment and to each and every problem.

He did not impose his views

"As is well known, Che's economic policies were carried out in the framework of the budgetary finance system. And there's one thing that says a lot about his personal qualities, which is that he didn't impose his views but submitted them for discussion. In the magazine *Nuestra Industria Económica*, which at that time was one of the three publications we had in the Ministry of Industry, there were articles on the economic accounting and the budgetary finance systems, both from defenders and opponents.

"He also created a policy on scientific development and established institutes such as ICIDCA, compelling us to come up with the personnel and resources required from what little we had.

"Che founded a Vice Ministry of Technological Development, which aimed to promote science and technology, as well as a Vice Ministry of Industrial Construction. There was a lack of experience in the country. Nevertheless, factories were built such as the domestic utensils plant in Santa Clara, which was up and running in two years, and the textile mills of Gibara and Alquízar.

"Only a genius could oversee all that, in the midst of the blockade, of sabotage, of counterrevolution, of the lack of trained personnel in everything.

"Che had no special background for this task. He was a doctor, a guerrilla fighter, and everything he did began when he was assigned there. In addition, he had political, military, and international responsibilities, a host of things. But one of his hours at the ministry was the equivalent of months of work.

"When you look back at that time, and see this as whole, you say: 'This was the work of a giant.'

1. Guanahacabibes was a work camp for administrators in the Ministry of Industry who committed serious infractions. Going there for a period of time was voluntary political punishment. If an administrator refused to go, he would be removed from his position. After completing a period of time there, persons were reinstated in their old post.

'CHE GUEVARA WAS ENERGETICALLY DEVOTED TO ANTI-IMPERIALIST SOLIDARITY'

Interview with Manuel Piñeiro on Che Guevara's internationalist missions

by Luis Suárez Salazar, Ivette Zuazo, and Ana María Pellón

Below is an interview with Manuel Piñeiro, member of the Central Committee of the Communist Party of Cuba, that was featured in a special 30th anniversary issue of the magazine *Tricontinental* published in Havana by the Organization of Solidarity with the Peoples of Africa, Asia, and Latin America.

During the 1960s, Piñeiro was the head of the General Directorate of Intelligence of the Ministry of the Interior of Cuba, which among other things was in charge of relations with revolutionary movements in the Third World. The interview is reprinted by permission. Translation and footnotes are by the *Militant*. Due to its size, the interview was first published in two parts in *Militant* vol. 61, nos. 41 and 42, dated respectively Nov. 24 and Dec. 1, 1997.

A tremendous downpour broke out right as the tape recorder began. Jokes were in the air. "You're going to take my virginity away," our subject warned us, alluding to the fact that though he has met with journalists before, this is the first time in 30 years he has agreed to be interviewed about Che Guevara.

He has received many requests from Cuban and foreign journalists. The reason is that Manuel Piñeiro, nicknamed Red Beard in the 1960s by friend and foe alike, is a key witness in reconstructing Che's entire internationalist course, from 1959 up to his murder in Bolivia in 1967.

During those years Piñeiro was no less than the head of the General Directorate of Intelligence of the Ministry of the Interior of Cuba, which among other responsibilities, was in charge of relations with revolutionary movements in the Third World. Insurgencies were then in full bloom. Among Che's multiple tasks within the leadership of the Cuban revolution were promoting anti-imperialist solidarity and prepar-

BOHEMIA

TRICONTINENTAL

Above, Cubans and international supporters rally in Havana to support nationalization of imperialist-owned properties in Cuba, August 1960. Banners include quote from Nicaraguan revolutionary Augusto Cesar Sandino. **At right,** Manuel Piñeiro with Che Guevara (right).

ing himself to fight in "other lands"—efforts he devoted himself to energetically. Piñeiro worked very closely with him in this.

Piñeiro earned the trust that got him this post in the Sierra Maestra primarily. He went there in May 1957 after making a request to the leadership of the July 26 Movement in Havana. Prior to that he had been one of the leaders of the Movement in his native province of Matanzas. From there he had to move to the capital, his cover blown due to his sabotage and propaganda activities. After organizing various arms shipments to the Sierra, he reached the eastern mountains.

There he joined Column no. 1 commanded by Fidel. In March 1958 he passed over to the column led by Raúl Castro, who founded the "Frank País" Second Eastern Front. There Piñeiro was made head of the Territorial Personnel and Inspection Directorate, the Intelligence Service, and the Rebel Police. He ended the war with the rank of commander. He participated in founding the Ministry of the Interior in 1961, and remained there until 1975. He served almost a decade as central leader of the Technical Vice Ministry; and later, as head of the General Directorate of National Liberation.

Beginning in 1975 he spent more than a decade and a half heading the Americas Department of the Central Committee of the Communist Party of Cuba. He has been a member of that committee since its establishment on October 3, 1965. That was the very day in which Fidel made public Che's farewell letter.

Today, at 64 years of age, with his beard and hair turned gray, Piñeiro has not abandoned his preference—or custom—for working into the early hours of the morning. He does so whether in the Central Committee building, which he enters every day shortly after noon, or in the simple terrace of his home, where we are now meeting. The normal work environment of the "distinguished" individual is revealed: mounds of publications and documents on Latin America cover the furniture; at the foot of a plastic table is a lamp; there is a hammock and lush greenery in the small yard. But one also has to say that amid the intense activity as a revolutionary, he has reserved a place for family: his wife, Chilean Marxist writer Marta Harnecker; Camila, their daughter; and his eldest son Manuel, who is a lawyer.

Almost four hours of discussion have gone by and he is as fresh as when he started. He has fallen short in only one promise he made, to himself above all: to be brief. But he does not have to apologize for forgetting details; his memory is as sharp as ever.

He granted this interview after so many years not for himself, but as "my modest homage to Che Guevara."

Question: When and under what circumstances did you meet Che?

Answer: The first time I saw him was in passing, when our columns crossed after the battle of Pino del Agua (September 10, 1957). Through other combatants who had spoken of him with much respect and affection, I already knew he was a courageous and daring Argentine with a broad cultural background and solid political ideas.

Later I met him again in El Hombrito, another place in the Sierra Maestra, where his command post was located. It had an armory, bakery, and medical and dental services, in which he himself was the dentist, with a pair of pliers as his only instrument. Coincidentally it was the same date as today (June 10). I had a tremendous toothache, but when I went to find Che I heard shouts and moans, and I saw him working inside a peasant's mouth, pliers in hand, extracting a tooth. I told myself I'd never allow myself to fall into that man's hands. I don't believe I'll ever forget that image.

Question: Beyond that impact, what impression did you have of his personality?

Answer: He gave the impression of serenity, of a great deal of self-confidence, which inspired respect. At first he could seem serious or introverted, but once personal contact was established he became very communicative, with a sharp sense of humor, often laced with irony. I believe that some comrades, with a different psychology, different cultural backgrounds, and different personal traits did not understand his jokes, saying they were "Argentine," with a very biting edge. In reality, his jokes often had a certain critical tone, but they were always courteous and educational, never meant to give offense to any comrade, always appealing to their personal honor.

Question: After the triumph of the revolution, when did you meet him again?

Answer: On May Day 1959 he attended the march in Santiago de Cuba, capital of the former province of Oriente. At the time I was in charge there militarily, so I met him and we held a meeting in my office in the Moncada garrison. But my close ties with Che began in the second half of 1959.

TRICONTINENTAL

There was revolutionary ferment throughout Latin America in 1960s. **At left,** peasants demonstrate in Peru, 1964. **Right,** Guevara with Jorge Ricardo Masetti, who organized 1963 guerilla effort in Argentina in collaboration with Che. Most revolutionary leaders from other countries who passed through Havana met with Guevara.

Solidarity with revolutionary struggles

Question: Was that when you began to work together in activities connected with solidarity with revolutionary struggles in the Third World?

Answer: Yes. That year I transferred from Oriente to Havana, to join in founding the security and intelligence structures leading up to the creation, on June 6, 1961, of the Ministry of the Interior [MININT], which Comrade Ramiro Valdés headed. These incipient structures, and later the Technical Vice Ministry of MININT—which I was assigned to lead—were also responsible for attending to revolutionary and political leaders from other countries of the Third World, who came to learn from the experience of the Cuban revolution. Naturally, they wanted to talk to the revolution's principal leaders, above all Fidel and Che. Che made available the little time that he had, above all the nights, as he used to do with any peasant or rebel combatant in the Sierra who wanted to speak with him. The meetings with those leaders, the majority them from Latin America and the Caribbean, extended into the early morning, and sometimes to sunrise. They were held in safe houses, in Che's offices first in the National Institute of Agrarian Reform, and then the National Bank and the Ministry of Industry, and occasionally at his house.

Question: Did you participate in all of them?

Answer: Almost all. If not me, then some other comrade attending to the visitor.

Question: What do you remember most about those meetings?

Answer: Invariably they were "presided over" by a thermos of hot water, a sipping tube, maté, and a cigar in Che's mouth. I was always struck by his capacity to listen, his respect for the opinions of the person speaking, even when these did not coincide with his own views. This did not signify, however, that he didn't express his point of view, with very convincing arguments. Even without his visitor realizing it, Che could create a climate of relaxation, trust, and a fraternal spirit, which enabled both of them to speak in a direct and frank way.

Although he remained on top of the political situation and the emergence of revolutionary movements in the Third World, especially Latin America, Che would read all the material we had about the political, economic, and social conditions of the country in question prior to the meetings. It was inexcusable not to have a map laid out on the table, because as a man of detail, he liked to make inquiries analyzing the geography, the topography of the territory, the characteristics of the rural population, the forms of land ownership, social struggles and their antecedents, the movements of peasants, workers, and students, the political organizations, the intellectual world. He was extremely meticulous in seeking facts and figures on these topics.

In a pedagogical manner, free of schemas and dogmas, he would explain the Cuban revolutionary experience, and within it not just his own experience, but that of the other leaders, like Fidel and Raúl Castro, Juan Almeida, Camilo Cienfuegos. He did not fail to point out to the visitor that one must take advantage of the smallest opening that existed for legal activity, but without creating illusions, keeping fully in mind the indispensable need to accumulate the maximum amount of forces, and to prepare oneself militarily to confront the repression of the popular and revolutionary movement, to the degree that it became a dangerous challenge to the ruling system. Likewise, he would warn them of the probability of an aggressive reaction by imperialism to the advance of the revolutionary struggles. Sometimes he would also enter into philosophical and cultural matters.

QUESTION: Could you mention some of the Latin American leaders who came to make contact with him?

ANSWER: It's impossible to mention them all, but among the many, I recall the Nicaraguans Carlos Fonseca, Tomás Borge, Rodolfo Romero, and the former officer in the Somocista Army, Somarriba, who headed an attempt at armed struggle in Nicaragua—which was eventually defeated and in which Cuban comrades Omelio Hernández and Marcelo Fernández died. I also recall the Guatemalans Turcios Lima, Yon Sosa, Rolando Ramírez, Pablo Monzanto, and Julio Cáceres (Patojo), a very dear friend of Che's. There were the Peruvians Luis de la Puente Uceda, Héctor Béjar, and Javier Heraud; the Peronists William Cooke and Alicia Eguren; the Colombians Fabio Vázquez (who would later head the National Liberation Army—ELN), the liberal guerrilla leader Franco, the La Rota brothers (founders of the Colombian Worker-Student Movement) and the general secretary of the CP in that country, Gilberto Vieira. There was also the secretary of the Uruguayan CP, Rodney Arismendi; the principal leaders of the Chilean Socialist and Communist parties, above all Salvador Allende, then a senator of the republic, and Jaime Barrios; the principal leaders of the Venezuelan CP, Fabricio Ojeda; and various Haitian and Dominican leaders.

In general, all the leaders of left-wing and Communist parties of the continent who passed through Havana, met with him. It should be recalled that Che participated in the Conference of Communist Parties of Latin America, held in Cuba in 1964.

QUESTION: Can it be said that ever since the triumph of the revolution, Cuba's policy of solidarity with Latin America began to converge with Che's idea of becoming a part of the battle for liberation in other countries of Latin America?

ANSWER: Two things should not be forgotten. As far back as *History Will Absolve Me* [1954] Fidel has pointed to the Latin Americanist thrust of the revolution. He himself had participated in the *Bogotazo*, in activities of solidarity with the struggle for the independence of Puerto Rico, for [Argentina's] sovereignty over the Malvinas Islands, for the recovery of the Panama Canal, and there was the failed expedition of Cayo Confite to overthrow the Dominican dictator Leónidas Trujillo.[1] In Che, Fidel met someone who already had the same determination; he was marked by the experience of the defeat of President Jacobo Arbenz in Guatemala in 1954.[2] In that country Che met many revolutionary leaders of the continent, which strengthened his anti-imperialist and Latin Americanist feelings and convictions.

The other thing to recall is that before leaving for Cuba on the *Granma*, Che raised with Fidel that as soon as he could be freed of his responsibilities with the Cuban revolution, and whenever the time was most opportune, he wanted to be free to join the revolutionary struggle in another country of Latin America, preferably Argentina. He was always alert to any opportunity that presented some perspective for the development of revolutionary armed struggle, such as Nicaragua, Venezuela, or Colombia. He was always interested in the possibility of being accepted as a participant in the struggles of other countries.

For example, as early as 1959, Che sent a Cuban emissary with a note to the anti-Somoza Nicaraguan Somarriba, expressing his willingness to join the struggle as soon as the guerrilla column was able to create the conditions in that country. The effort failed, to Che's sorrow.

QUESTION: How did Che conceive of the development and spread of the revolutionary struggle in Latin America?

ANSWER: His conception, rooted in the Cuban war of liberation, consisted in founding a *mother column*, composed of revolutionaries of various Latin American countries. Once the stage of survival was overcome, the combatants forged, the leadership cadres formed, then as this column developed and grew it would create the conditions for separating off other columns. In this way it would expand the battle to other countries of the continent; above all toward those that had united with imperialism to defeat the popular cause.

As the Cuban experience demonstrated, the original guerrilla nucleus, if it were well led, would be the *little motor* that through political and military action would set into motion the *big motor* of the masses. This was the basis of the continental and anti-imperialist conception of Che on revolutionary armed struggle. It is essentially a political and military conception based on the masses, in opposition to the interpretation that reduced things to the "guerrilla foco," a view that has been attributed to Che. He spoke of an insurrectional foco rooted in the masses, not a small group of armed men who act separate and apart from the popular movement and the people in general.

EDITORA POLITICA

Cuban volunteers training for internationalist mission in Bolivia in San Andrés, Pinar del Río, Cuba, fall 1966. Left to right: Joaquín, Braulio, Rolando, Urbano, Alejandro, Marcos, Benigno, Antonio, Che Guevara (Ramón), Miguel, Rubio. Goal was to advance revolutionary struggle through the Americas.

He also said that the guerrilla struggle could not develop in countries whose governments were the result of some form of elections, and where the possibilities of civic struggle had not been exhausted.

One basic idea of Che's should be stressed: all the conditions do not necessarily have to exist before the revolutionary struggle can begin; the struggle itself can create them as it develops.

Che is therefore not responsible for the oversimplifications of the Cuban experience and of his conceptions that were developed by various revolutionaries in Latin America, albeit with the best of intentions.

Question: Was Che's preference for Argentina at the root of the guerrilla effort commanded by his compatriot Jorge Ricardo Masetti in 1963? What was Che's role in that?

Answer: Che had known Masetti as a journalist in the Sierra Maestra. After January 1959 Masetti returned to Cuba; he carried out a few missions of support to the revolution in Algeria with the National Liberation Front (FLN). In addition he acquired some combat experience, attending military school in our country. Che then gave him the task of organizing a guerrilla column whose principal mission was to install itself in an area in Argentina along the border with Bolivia, specifically Salta, with the idea of Che himself joining as soon as a minimum of conditions was created, to use that as a base to lead the beginning of the armed struggle in Argentina. He paid special attention to the preparation of that detachment, named the Guerrilla Army of the Poor (EGP), which Masetti was to be part of together with other comrades, including the Cubans Hermes Peña (killed in action) and Alberto Castellanos, who fell prisoner and remained in Argentine jails for four years without their being able to discover his true nationality.

Question: When Masetti left for Salta he called himself "Segundo" [Number Two]. Was this an allusion to the fact that he was heading it only temporarily?

Answer: Yes, because Number One was Che. That's the significance of Masetti's pseudonym. Che wanted to be the initiator, but Fidel was able to persuade him to enter Argentina only after an advance group had created the conditions. In other words, Che would not be there during the most difficult and risky stage of any guerrilla movement, that of survival. During this stage the guerrilla unit depends fundamentally on its own forces.

This view has its precedent in the cadre policy Fidel developed in the Sierra Maestra. He always tried to preserve intermediate leaders who stood out as heads of columns. This policy was proven correct in our war. Fidel did not want to risk a cadre of Che's experience and continental stature during the first stage of the guerrilla struggle.

QUESTION: Nevertheless, that effort had Cuba's solidarity.

ANSWER: It was necessary to establish a base of logistical support beforehand on the Bolivian side, and several Cuban cadres were designated for this: Abelardo Colomé Ibarra (Furry), today a corps general of the army, and José María Martínez Tamayo (Papi) who would die several years later in the Bolivian guerrilla movement. They went to Bolivia to provide assistance to Masetti and his group, with the aid of the Peredo brothers and Rodolfo Saldaña (members of the Bolivian CP), in coordination with a group of comrades we sent to La Paz. Simultaneously, on Che's request the married couple William Cooke and Alicia Eguren were responsible for support work in Argentina, even though they did not know the plans totally, nor the eventual participation of Che in that guerrilla movement.

It's also necessary to recognize here the cooperation given at that time by the leadership of the Algerian FLN.

QUESTION: Masetti's insurgency was eventually discovered and almost all its members died or disappeared. What impact did this have on Che?

ANSWER: A deeply emotional and human impact. Comrades had been killed with whom he had been tied by many years of comradeship and struggle. As he said more than once, what upset him was the idea that while this was occurring he was here sitting in an office. When contact with Masetti was lost in April 1964, Che made all possible efforts to clarify the circumstances of those events, to learn if there were survivors, and in case they existed, to reorganize them. In those efforts he had the collaboration of William and Alicia. Since then, other Argentine friends have continued looking for the remains of Masetti and his comrades, trying to reconstruct the events, but up to now they have not been able to find indications of how that guerrilla effort ended and the circumstances of Masetti's death.

QUESTION: During that same period, Che paid close attention to the efforts at insurgency in Peru. Is it true that this country was an alternative evaluated by him prior to selecting Bolivia?

ANSWER: Argentina, Peru, Bolivia—all of these were part of his integrated plan of advancing his strategy of a continental revolution.

Parallel to the Salta operation, in January 1963 a group of Peruvian combatants led by Alain Elías, and among them Javier Heraud and Abraham Lamas, attempted to begin armed struggle, entering Peru through the zone of Puerto Maldonado, on the border with Bolivia. The young Peruvian poet Javier Heraud and other comrades were killed there. They had the support of various cadres of the Bolivian CP, especially the Peredo brothers, who provided them with logistical support and served as guides for their column to enter Peru from Bolivia. Years later the ELN[3] reinitiated the struggle under the leadership of Héctor Béjar. The guerrilla movements of Luis de la Puente Uceda and Guillermo Lobatón, leaders of the Movement of the Revolutionary Left (MIR), also emerged. Che had met with all these Peruvian leaders previously.

In other words, there was a certain degree of organization and a popular upsurge. Social struggles were going on, such as the land seizures led by Hugo Blanco. At the same time Peru was attractive to Che because it was closer to Argentina. Besides, in that period a democratic government existed in Bolivia, which had arisen out of the revolution of 1952, and it lasted until 1964. However, the guerrilla effort of the ELN, as well as those of the MIR, were destroyed. Luis de la Puente Uceda was killed (in November 1965) as well as Lobatón (in January 1966); Héctor Béjar was arrested in 1965 and the column he led was defeated. . . .

QUESTION: How did Che react to these reverses, which clearly postponed his continent-wide effort?

ANSWER: He seemed very impatient. He did not stop exploring the possibility of joining the armed struggle in other countries, such as Venezuela and Colombia. Nevertheless, favorable conditions did not exist to receive a revolutionary of his political and military stature, with all the consequences this would entail.

QUESTION: When did he begin thinking about

TRICONTINENTAL GRANMA

Left: Manuel Piñeiro (front, third from right) with Guevara at 1959 May Day celebration in Santiago, Cuba. **Right:** Fidel Castro reads Guevara's letter of farewell at meeting to introduce Central Committee of Communist Party of Cuba, Oct. 3, 1965.

Bolivia as a scene of battle and not just as a zone of support? Why did he decide on that country?

ANSWER: In 1964 Barrientos carried out a coup d'état in Bolivia and a period of intense repression was opened. At the same time, however, there was a movement of popular resistance, particularly by the miners and students. From that time on, Che began to watch the unfolding of events. Two years later, while he was in Tanzania, Che decided to send Papi to Bolivia to evaluate the situation. The latter confirmed Che's view that this was the only viable option, in the sense that there existed the minimum political conditions and there were experienced Bolivian cadres, who had taken part in assisting Masetti and the Peruvian guerrillas. That is, there were steeled individuals who were prepared, politically and ideologically, to give solidarity to any revolutionary movement that arose in the area.

QUESTION: How did the Bolivian effort fit into Che's continental strategy?

ANSWER: In his view, that guerrilla effort was to have become a school for forming Latin American cadres, above all from the Southern Cone—among them Argentines—which would help extend the armed struggle to neighboring countries. At the same time, it would enable him to accumulate political and military forces and wait for the most opportune occasion to continue the struggle toward his native country.

This would depend on the development and growth of the *mother column* established in Bolivia. Without that, it would not be possible to continue toward Argentina, where a bloody military dictatorship had also been installed, supported by the United States and repudiated by the most combative sectors of the Argentine people.

In a realistic manner, Che calculated that if, beginning with Bolivia, other guerrilla columns arose and evolved, composed of combatants of various countries of the Southern Cone, this would provoke as a reaction an alliance with the governments and armies of the neighboring countries, supported by imperialism. Such a development would contribute to spreading the revolutionary armed struggle in the region, which would turn into a scene of cruel, long, and difficult battles that sooner or later would lead to Yankee intervention. It would therefore become another Vietnam, as he called for in his historic "Message to the Peoples of the World" through the Tricontinental.[4]

QUESTION: Did the original idea and the plan for Bolivia come entirely from Che?

ANSWER: Yes, the selection of the place, the combatants, the design, and the preparation of the plan were all conceived by him. Naturally, Fidel offered all possible support and cooperation. He again raised that Che should not be part of the advance forces, but should instead go once things were in place and a minimum set of conditions had been created: logistics, weapons, an urban support network, and the incorporation of Latin American cadres, in particular Bolivians, as well as their training, adaptation to the terrain, and so on. In short, he proposed that the guerrilla movement should first pass through the stage of survival. But by now Che was eager to begin the struggle, above all in a country such as this, bordering the one he wanted to take the revolutionary battle to: Argentina.

In addition, from the psychological point of view he felt very pressed by the passage of years. He knew better than anyone that there were elementary physical conditions that were indispensable for leading a guerrilla movement. He knew it would not be easy to carry out the plan at the conjuncture Latin America was then going through, with the United States undertaking the demobilizing Alliance for Progress, and the whole counterinsurgency campaign of supporting the regimes of the area, which it supplied with arms, financial resources, and military training. They wanted to prevent at all costs the spread of the Cuban revolution's example.

QUESTION: It has been said that after publication of his farewell letter, Che felt he had made a moral commitment not to return to Cuba, or not to take on a visible post again in the leadership of the revolution. . . .

ANSWER: In my opinion, with or without a farewell letter, Che's plan was unalterable. He was determined to fulfill what he had laid out as his historic and strategic objective: to spread the anti-imperialist struggle throughout the continent.

QUESTION: If we discount Ciro Bustos, only one Argentine remained in the Bolivian guerrilla movement, Tania. What do you think was the explanation for the almost insignificant presence of Argentines there?

ANSWER: Bustos was a liaison who had a series of connections and relations given him by Che, so that contact could be made with Argentines of different organizations and brought to the zone where he was operating in Bolivia. After Bustos was taken prisoner and turned informer—offering information and drawings identifying Che and the guerrillas—Argentina was "frozen." Remember too that when the army discovered the guerrilla base, the whole plan unfolded in an accelerated way. The guerrilla unit had to stay on the move constantly, and at that stage it became very difficult to maintain contact with the urban base and contact with those outside the country.

Had this not occurred, I believe, then when Che's presence in Bolivia became known, many cadres and combatants from various revolutionary forces on the continent would have looked for a way to come and participate. Che's call to action exerted a great influence on many revolutionaries inside and outside Latin America.

QUESTION: What merit is there to the story spread around the world that Cuba's political leadership abandoned Che in Bolivia and did not provide him the support necessary for the success of his operation?

ANSWER: From the very beginning of the Cuban revolution—and much earlier, going back to our first wars of independence—the empire has practiced a strategy of trying to divide the revolutionary forces. First it circulated the story that the disappearance of Camilo was the result and consequence of differences within the revolutionary leadership;[5] later it spoke of supposed differences between Raúl and Fidel; and later between Fidel and Che. In this way it mounted a whole campaign of disinformation that has lasted up to the present, to try to sow confusion not only in Cuba but in the Latin American and world revolutionary movement, and in international public opinion. One of the centerpieces of these campaigns is the supposed abandonment of Che's guerrilla movement, which is based on questioning why we didn't send military reinforcements to support him and to help him break the Bolivian army's encirclement.

Anyone who knows the laws of guerrilla warfare is aware that in the initial and most difficult phase, the guerrilla column is compelled to be on the move constantly to avoid the ambushes of the enemy army, especially if it is at a disadvantage. In such a phase, the guerrilla unit depends on its own forces and the backing it can receive from the urban network, which at that time had been hard hit. Therefore, it would not have been such an easy task to send—to use their term—military reinforcements. It's pure fantasy.

QUESTION: And is it also a fantasy to compare, as has been done, the supposed lack of support to Che with the successful Cuban efforts to get its officers out of Venezuela?[6]

ANSWER: With absolute knowledge and responsibility I can state that in Venezuela the Communist Party, the MIR [Movement of the Revolutionary Left], and other revolutionary forces, although they had suffered some defeats, maintained clandestine structures and operational facilities that helped make possible the patient and meticulous organization of the operation to get these comrades out. Those circumstances did not exist in Bolivia.

QUESTION: Returning to 1965, you were very closely involved in the preparations of the Cuban internationalist mission in the Congo led by Che that year. In your judgment, what did that stage represent for him in relation to his final strategic plan?

ANSWER: At that time, although there was certainly a revolutionary upsurge on a world scale, headed by the heroic Vietnamese people, and under the impact of the Cuban revolution, nevertheless the minimum conditions for Che to materialize his plan in Latin America still did not exist. Based on this, and on the request for aid that had been made of Cuba, through Che, by the leadership of the Supreme Revolutionary Council of the Congo, Fidel proposed that the most useful thing Che could do was to head up the group of Cuban military advisers who would be heading off to that African country. The aim would be to allow Che to gain time while accumulating experience, getting himself ready again, and at the same time preparing some of the Cuban cadres and combatants who would accompany him later to Bolivia.

Che viewed the Congo stage as a stepping stone, an intermediate phase to prepare himself for his definitive goal. There he would wait for the evolution of developments in Latin America to create favorable political conditions to carry out his strategic plans. So much so that as he was leaving the Congo, Che asked Harry Villegas, Carlos Coello, and José María Martínez Tamayo if they were willing to continue the struggle together with him, in another country, a struggle that would be long, complex, and difficult. These comrades were later part of the Bolivian guerrilla movement under the pseudonyms of Pombo, Tuma, and Ricardo.

QUESTION: What was the role of the vice ministry you headed in the delicate operations to get Che and his comrades to Africa, later return to Cuba, and then go to Bolivia?

ANSWER: Our department was in charge of the entire technical and operational preparation for the Congo mission, supplying the documents, travel itineraries, and false identities. Starting with our embassy in Tanzania, we constituted a support group in charge of seeking information and cooperation in the shipment of logistics from that country to Che's base in the Congo, the training of the radio operators, as well as other forms of contact and communication with Che.

On Fidel's instructions, the Technical Vice Ministry of the Ministry of the Interior gave support to Che on everything he requested in relation to the future mission in Bolivia. We supplied the documents, the false passports, the information he requested on various situations in Bolivia, the training in different specialized areas, such as communications and conspiratorial methods.

All the technical details were prepared by our officials, but each step was analyzed and approved by Che: the routes chosen and who would take them; how to pass unnoticed through airports, airport characteristics and border checks, the thoroughness of immigration checks, at what times and on what days was there less vigilance by the authorities. Toward this end a study was made on the operational, border control, and immigration situation, and the methods applied by the counterintelligence forces of the countries Che and the other combatants would be passing through.

Some day, at the right moment, this story will have to be told in more detail, and recognition given to the comrades who worked on that operation, and not a single name will be omitted. More than 140 Cubans went to Africa, and more than 20 to Bolivia, without being detected by the organs of Yankee espionage, nor by the security apparatus of the countries they were passing through. The work was carried out with great meticulousness, professionalism, strict division of labor, and above all with great motivation since it involved Che and those who accompanied him.

We lived through those days in great tension; I'm speaking for the entire team in charge of these tasks. We knew that a single error of any type could cost the life of a participant in the mission. These were hours of anxiety and permanent vigilance, until we received confirmation of the arrival of Che and the rest of the group at their destination. I will never forget those moments, nor will any of the comrades who carried out that difficult internationalist task in anonymity.

QUESTION: What was Che's frame of mind in the months between his return from the Congo and his departure for Bolivia? He came from a defeat in Africa. . . .

ANSWER: A defeat whose causes he explained, making a self-criticism besides, as he was accustomed to doing given his personality and standard of ethics. But one must always remember that he went to the Congo to transmit his experience and to advise, not to lead that war of national liberation. Once he was there he came up against the cultural and religious traditions, the differences among the Congolese leaders, the lack of combat experience. Psychologically this was a very difficult situation to confront, above all for our combatants who were steeled in battle, with experience of struggle, and who wanted not only to advise but to participate in direct combat against the enemy. It was not easy, understandably.

For that reason, Che directly took part in combat, and was prepared to accept the final consequences of his acts. Nevertheless, the decisions taken by the Congolese leadership and by the governments of Africa created a conjuncture where there was no alternative but to organize his departure from the Congo and that of all the other comrades.

With respect to Che's morale before leaving for Bolivia, he was like a child with a new toy. He was euphoric, happy, because he was with the group he had selected, and by then they had already been trained. He acted in a very fraternal manner with the comrades, although he was also very disciplined and demanding. They followed a plan of rigorous physical, military, and psychological training; reading of documents on that country, learning the Quechua language, mathematics classes. He was very much concerned with raising the cultural level of the combatants under him.

QUESTION: In April 1967, when Che was already in Bolivia, a supplement to our magazine published his "Message to the Peoples of the World." Nevertheless, according to some versions, this was not written in Bolivia but in Cuba. What can you tell us about this?

ANSWER: I believe that's basically correct, that he wrote it during the time he was at the training camp in Pinar del Río province, before his departure for Bolivia in November 1966.

QUESTION: It's noteworthy that while he devoted so many intellectual and practical efforts at internationalism, he didn't attend the historic Solidarity Conference of the Peoples of Asia, Africa, and Latin America, held in January 1966. What was the reason?

ANSWER: He couldn't attend because while the Tricontinental Conference was being held, he was in Tanzania. But while there he received all the materials and an assessment of the meeting.

QUESTION: What was the impact on you of Che's farewell letter?

ANSWER: I already knew of it before it was read by Fidel in the presentation of the first Central Committee of the Communist Party in October 1965. Nevertheless, every time I hear or read it, I'm deeply moved and it brings back many memories both of Che and of his comrades, since I knew all of them and had close personal and working ties with some of them.

QUESTION: The last time you saw Che alive, did you think it would be the last time?

ANSWER: I saw him in the early morning hours of the day he went to the airport to go join the guerrilla struggle in Bolivia. It was in a safe house where he held, I believe, his last conversation with Fidel. Raúl Castro and Vilma Espín were also there. Fidel and Che were sitting on a sofa, talking there by themselves, in low voices, for a very long time.

I didn't think this would be the last time I would see him, although those of us involved in this type of struggle know that in it one either triumphs or dies. We were very optimistic, and very confident in the determination, will, and capacity of Che, of the Cubans who accompanied him, and of the Bolivians, who had proven themselves in other tasks, to attain their objective and be able to deal capably with all the difficulties they would encounter. In reality, the Bolivian guerrilla movement was able to carry out a number of successful military actions, inflicting casualties on the army's soldiers and taking prisoners.

Che did not have a mystical view of death, as has been attributed to him. Had he survived alone or with another combatant he would have tried to reorganize the guerrilla unit and continue the battle. He was not a man to give his life easily to his enemies, nor did he have an inclination to be a martyr. Proof of this is that even when he was wounded and his rifle put out of action, he tried to escape from the encirclement to meet up again with his men. He never felt defeated or demoralized. He defended his ideas with his own flesh and blood, unconcerned about whether he might give his life in the effort.

QUESTION: Did Che say goodbye to you? What kind of farewell was it?

ANSWER: He did so in the safe house I mentioned. He was happy, smiling. He was finally heading off to his long-awaited goal.

It was a simple farewell; he was not very effusive. Che carried his emotions inside himself; one had to know how to decipher them. But as always, the expression on his face transmitted great force and conviction.

QUESTION: How did you learn of Che's death?

ANSWER: By a radiophoto I received on October 10, where Che's body was shown in the hospital laundry room. I called Fidel and he came to my house. I remember Fidel's expression, one of doubt. He saw some resemblance to Che in the photo, but was not completely convinced it was him. He headed home, and he was there with Comrade Celia Sánchez when I brought him a second radiophoto I'd received, which left no doubt it was Che. That moment remains etched in my memory like a photograph that I'll never forget. There was a great silence in the house. Fidel sent Comrade Celia to find Aleida, Che's wife, who was conducting research in the Escambray mountains, to give her the news personally. He then called other comrades in the party leadership and began to give instructions on how the news should be transmitted, and to prepare our people for the harsh news.

It was a tremendous blow. But on those revolutionary missions, one leaves one's life under one's pillow.

QUESTION: How long after that did you learn there were survivors?

ANSWER: Shortly afterward, when Pombo, Urbano, and the now-traitor Benigno succeeded in breaking the encirclement, and when Inti Peredo, in particular, established contact with some members of the Bolivian Communist Party and the ELN [National Liberation Army] who took them to the Chilean border. I always remember with great affection the role played by Salvador Allende, at the time president of the Chilean senate, who despite criticism from the right wing, offered his full support and protection to the three survivors. He informed our ambassador in France, Baudilio Castellanos, that he would accompany the three survivors to Tahiti. Our ambassador flew there, and brought them to France, and then to Cuba.

Equally, the collaboration offered by the Chilean Communist and Socialist parties should be noted, as well as that of Beatriz Allende and many other comrades, among them the journalist Elmo Catalán, who would later die in combat together with Inti Peredo, trying to reinitiate the armed struggle in Bolivia.

QUESTION: Recently you were able to read the testimony of the Chilean Manuel Cabieses, published in the magazine *Liberación*, about the arrival of Che's diary in Cuba. What is your opinion of it?

ANSWER: It's very objective. Cabieses is a serious journalist, rigorous in his analyses and journalistic works. In addition, he is a very consistent revolutionary, with a fraternal attitude of solidarity to Cuba and revolutionary movements in Latin America.

This question reminds me of the participation of various comrades in the publication of the Diary in other languages: the Italian Feltrinelli, a friend of the Cuban revolution and an admirer of Che; the Frenchman François Maspero; Arnaldo Orfila, of Siglo XXI in Mexico; and the staff of the magazine *Ramparts* in the United States. Also the publishers in other countries who, under the coordination of Rolando Rodríguez, then-president of the Cuban Book Institute, made an extraordinary effort to publish the Diary in Cuba and the entire world before the U.S. secret services could publish a falsified version, as they wanted to. That battle was won.

QUESTION: What is your opinion of the biographies of Che that have recently appeared?

ANSWER: I have not read them all, although I have seen some comments published in newspapers in Latin America where one of these biographies in particular tries to present Che as purely a cultural symbol, above all among the youth, stripping him of his political and ideological message and of his example. Some—because not all of them present a negative balance sheet—emphasize that all of Che's economic, political, and military ideas have failed, that they are out of date, and that the road taken by the Cuban revolution has gone against his ideas.

In my opinion, if the Cuban revolution had abandoned Che's ideas, it would not continue being—as it is—a bastion of anti-imperialist and anticapitalist struggles that are taking place in the world, and of the fight for socialism. Even in the difficult circumstances of economic, political, and ideological aggression by imperialism, the Cuban people maintain the heroism Che summoned them to, and that they are summoned to every day by Fidel, who Che called his "teacher and guide."

The proof that the ideas, thought, actions, and example of Che have not failed and that they project the future, is that there is an ever growing and conscious interest both in Cuba and the world to study and interpret his works, recovering the essence of his ideas and analyzing the differences between the historic moment he lived in and the present.

In many countries, the consumer societies have sought to turn him into a piece of merchandise. Nevertheless, the image and example of Che rises above these attempts, much to the discomfort of the triumphalists of neoliberalism and the powerful in this world.

To try to reduce him to a cultural symbol is a vulgar simplification. I do not believe that the attraction and solidarity he evokes today among young people around the world, within the revolutionary movement, and in progressive and democratic sectors of the world are a result of this narrow perception of Che's legacy. Rather, they see him as a man with tremendous moral force, very honest, sensitive, human, capable of acting on his ideas, as a symbol of internationalism and anti-imperialism, of solidarity, of genuine socialism. In short, Che is seen as an example for the current and future generations, who will see in him a banner of revolutionary intransigence, of moral values, of social justice.

I believe that as long as there are oppressed and oppressors, social injustice, and imperialist domination, and as long as there is also hope for a just and fraternal world of solidarity among human beings and peoples, the ideas and example of Che will endure.

Therefore I agree with what Fidel said on October 12, 1987, at the event commemorating the 20th anniversary of the death in combat of Che and his comrades, "Che is more alive than ever, has more influence than ever, and is a more powerful opponent of imperialism than ever."

---

1. The *Bogotazo* was a popular uprising in Bogotá, Colombia in 1948. Castro was in Bogotá to help organize a Latin American student congress, and he participated in the uprising.

In 1947, an expedition was organized from Cuba to overthrow the Trujillo dictatorship in the Dominican Republic. It was aborted when the expeditionaries were dispersed by the Cuban army at Cayo Confite. Fidel Castro was a participant.

2. Seeking to crush political and social struggles in Guatemala accompanying a limited land reform initiated by the regime of Jacobo Arbenz, mercenary forces backed by the CIA invaded the country in 1954 to oust the government. Arbenz refused to arm the people and resigned, and a right-wing dictatorship took over. Among those volunteering to fight the imperialist-organized attack was Ernesto Guevara, who had been drawn to Guatemala by the upsurge in struggle there.

3. National Liberation Army of Peru.

4. Guevara's "Message to the Tricontinental," written in 1966, called for creating "two, three . . . many Vietnams." It is printed in *Pombo: A Man of Che's 'Guerrilla.'*

5. Camilo Cienfuegos was a Rebel Army commander who became chief of staff in January 1959. He died October 28, 1959, when his plane was lost over sea.

6. In 1967 several leading Cuban volunteers were in Venezuela, assisting in the armed struggle against the U.S.-supported regime in that country. Most were able to return to Cuba after the guerrillas were defeated.

'I AM THE DAUGHTER OF AN INTERNATIONALIST'

Interview with Aleida Guevara March

by Mario Jorge Muñoz

Below we reprint a major excerpt from an interview with Aleida Guevara March, daughter of Ernesto Che Guevara. The interview, by Mario Jorge Muñoz, appeared in the June 15, 1997, issue of *Juventud Rebelde*, the weekly paper of the Union of Young Communists of Cuba. Reprinted by permission. Translation is by the *Militant*.

My mother taught me from the time I was very little to know my father's ideals, his concerns, his ambitions as a revolutionary. And I have tried to follow that line in my life. In his letter of farewell to us, his children, he was asking us to strive to master technology, which enables one to master nature. He also told us to always study as much as we could, to never tire of it, because therein lies the possibility to best help humanity.

BRIDGET ELTON

MARTIN KOPPEL

Above, Cuban volunteer construction workers in Bluefields, Nicaragua, during revolution there. Internationalist missions "completed my education," said Aleida Guevara, shown **at right** speaking at conference on legacy of Che Guevara held at the University of Havana in October.

He asked that we should feel within ourselves the pain inflicted on any man anywhere in the world. I am the daughter of an internationalist. And that is the least I can give to humanity.

I cannot deny that my father had a certain influence in my choice of medicine as a profession. He was a doctor. But I believe that my decision was a little more selfish. As I grow older I want people to care about me not just because I am my father's daughter. I am always grateful for that, but such affection is not on account of me. As a human being I also need warmth and tenderness.

Medicine is a very humane profession. One in which, if you conduct yourself adequately, you can receive mountains of thanks. As a pediatrician I receive on a daily basis something better: the smiles of children. All the gold in the world cannot buy that. The feeling that you are doing something well, and that people care about you because you are their doctor, no matter whose daughter you are, is indescribable. I think this was the decisive reason I chose this profession.

Reprinted from *Militant* vol. 61, no. 43, Dec. 8, 1997.

My two internationalist missions as a doctor were tremendous experiences. They completed my education, above all because they confirmed that socialism is the only road possible for us. After living one year in Nicaragua and two years in Angola, I believe that if socialism were to disappear in Cuba, everything would be lost and we would become what Nicaragua, Guatemala, El Salvador, or Africa are today.

There are those who have looked at me in a different way and tried to be sweet, tender, and affectionate with us, because our father was not here and wasn't going to be here any more. And these people felt a commitment to him to give us everything they could on a human level. Sometimes spoiling us a bit, too. Other people felt a commitment to see that we, his children, became better every single day. On occasion, they would push us to the limit. Without realizing that we were normal, everyday children.

It was a much smaller group of people who treated us simply as regular human beings, genetic accidents of an extraordinary man and a very fine woman, nothing more.

I got to know that these were all expressions of the respect and admiration of the Cuban people and of those persons toward my father. That is, I got such treatment because I was an extension of him. People would focus their concern, their love, their demands, in his children. But these were always expressions of love. Very rarely have I felt anything else.

I believe that is why I like the song by Ana Belén, "Derroche" [outpouring] so much. Because all my life I have received an outpouring of love. Ever since I was born, simply, without having done anything to deserve it, I have felt tremendous tenderness from the Cuban people. People know me as the daughter of that extraordinary man. That's a little heavy for one person, but I have always felt the beautiful side of it.

One time, talking to my brother Camilo, I told him how much we would be able to learn from our father, how much we would be able to discuss with him, how many things he would be able to clarify. Camilo looked at me and said, "If he were alive, he would not be our father."

And Camilo was right. Because had he triumphed in Bolivia, he would certainly have continued toward the south, which was his objective. Because he never renounced being an Argentine. And the north of Argentina awaited him. I realize that. But it angers me, it pains me that a man with my father's capacity of thought and action died so young. I believe he would have been of much use in Cuba.

A few days ago I was talking to someone from France. He told me that if the example of my father had served a useful purpose, then many people like Che would exist in the world, but he didn't know of any. I answered that neither of us was in the position of saying there are not thousands of people like Che in the world. But he should also not forget that Ernesto Guevara met a Fidel Castro, that he met a group of men determined to make a real revolution.

That Che Guevara had the opportunity of being with the Cuban people, and that the Cuban people supported him up to the final consequences so he could carry out his dream. I then told him that perhaps there are thousands of Ches in the world, but they have not had the opportunity to make themselves known.

It is very interesting, for example, to see the young people in Italy, who have no relation to my father, or people in Spain, who are concerned about knowing my father directly from us. That is a sign that there really are people in the world who very much want to do something more, to not remain trapped in the consumer society, and to try to help one's fellow beings. That for me is a tremendous encouragement.

I believe that Che is a banner in the world, a banner of dignity, power, and courage. The fact that his image presides over the Fourteenth World Festival of Youth and Students is something he earned, because unfortunately he died a young man, 39 years old, and he will remain young forever.

If we can really get to know him more and if we carry a little of him inside of us, then that young man who gave us such a complete example of a man of the 21st century met his fundamental objective in life. Because we would be capable of being better human beings, the human beings of the future that he wanted. And society, humanity would therefore live much better.

'URBANO' SPEAKS ON EXPERIENCES WITH CHE IN BOLIVIA

Interview with Leonardo Tamayo

Below we reprint an interview with Leonardo Tamayo that appeared in the magazine *Tricontinental*, published in Havana by the Organization of Solidarity with the Peoples of Africa, Asia, and Latin America, in a special issue devoted to Ernesto Che Guevara. As a peasant youth in Cuba's Sierra Maestra, Tamayo joined the Rebel Army in Cuba in 1957 and served in Guevara's column. He fought with Che in Bolivia under the *nomme de guerre* Urbano, and later carried out internationalist missions in Nicaragua and Angola. Reprinted by permission. Translation and footnotes are by the *Militant.*

Leonardo Tamayo, known as "Urbano" in the Bolivian guerrilla unit, is one of the three Cuban survivors who escaped and returned to Cuba after Che's death. Tamayo met the Heroic Guerrilla for the first time at the age of 15 when he joined the Rebel Army in the Sierra Maestra, remaining with his commander as aide and bodyguard after 1959. He was with Che in Bolivia from November 1966 until October 1967.

GRANMA

MILITANT/RUSSELL JOHNSON

At top, Cuban survivors of the Bolivia campaign are interviewed by Cuban paper *Granma* Oct. 1, 1969. From left, Urbano, Harry Villegas (Pombo), and Dariel Alarcón (Benigno). Leonardo Tamayo, **right,** speaks at Auckland University in New Zealand, June 1996.

The journalist José Mayo includes a long and lively interview with Leonardo Tamayo in his book *With Che in Cuba and Bolivia*, soon to be released by the Cuban publishing house Capitán San Luis. We are reproducing four excerpts from that book: the first time Tamayo spoke with Commander Guevara; the discussion between Che and Bolivian Communist Party leader Mario Monje; the capture of the Samaipata barracks, and the news of Che's murder.

The first encounter

Through other guerrillas of peasant origin who I met in the Sierra Maestra, I'd begun to know about the audacity and courage in battle of the Argentine Ernesto Guevara. I knew he had been a *Granma* expeditionary,[1] and that because of his way of speaking he was called Che.

The rebels used to say that Che had a lot of guts because he always faced the enemy standing up,

Reprinted from *Militant* vol. 61, no. 44, Dec. 15, 1997.

without fear of bullets. One day I asked him why he fought on his feet, since it was more dangerous. He answered me that he had once been shot in the foot, and that if he'd been lying down the bullet would have got him in the head. He told me this a few months after I joined his command-post squad in Column no. 4.

What I had heard about Che made me picture him as a hero of legends, and that's why I wanted to be with him in battle. So I spoke with Lalo Sardiñas, and told him I wanted to fight alongside Che. He agreed. Then I went to Altos de Conrado, where they had told me I would find Che. When I saw him for the first time I didn't think it was Che, because I had imagined him to be very different physically. At that time he was really thin and smoked a pipe.

Since I had been told by some people that Che wasn't very talkative, I decided not to try to speak to him. Fidel had already named him a commander and head of Column no. 4. The first person I met who was under Che's direct command in Altos de Conrado was Hugo del Río. When he learned I had been fighting with Lalo Sardiñas he took me to see Che. Che looked at me and asked: "And what are *you* doing here?!"

Meeting between Che and Monje

Soon after we were settled in this place [the Main Camp, eight kilometers from the Ñancahuazú farm in Bolivia], on December 31, 1966, Che met with Mario Monje, general secretary of the Bolivian Communist Party, at Camp no. 1. Guido Peredo, Coello, René Martínez Tamayo, and I were with Che. When Monje saw Che he said, "Jesus, Che, look how skinny you are!" And Che shot back: "Jesus, Monje, look how paunchy you are!"

That's how they greeted each other. They talked for a long time about different things and then started discussing the armed struggle in Bolivia.

The last part of the conversation is engraved in my mind as though it were a tape recording.

Che said to Monje:

"Well, Monje, the moment we've been waiting for so much has come. It's fallen to you to play a part in the history of Bolivia's liberation. You'll be the second in command of the guerrilla force and the political officer."

He answered Che:

"Look, Che, I won't permit a foreigner to lead the armed struggle in my country. You must hand over the military and political command to me. You can be my adviser."

Che's response wasn't long in coming.

"Look, Monje, I don't like the role of adviser in this struggle because I believe it would mean shirking responsibilities somewhat, and I've never liked to do that."

Monje again replied to Che:

"Che, if it were any other country, I would carry your knapsack. But in my country, I can't permit a foreigner to lead the armed struggle."

With a firm and determined voice, Che put Monje in his place:

"Monje, that's a false conception of internationalism. It's as though I were in Argentina, in the situation you're in with me, and Fidel arrived. I would immediately subordinate myself to him because he knows more than I do."

Monje made a dismissive gesture and said,

"Che, I would not hand over command even if it were Lenin."

Che then asked him in a sarcastic voice:

"And if it were Malinovsky?"[2]

Monje was quiet for a few minutes, then suddenly blurted out:

"Che, you know that the CIA is powerful. At any moment they can have an agent infiltrate our ranks and they'll know right away that I'm not the commander, but just a puppet."

Che finally understood Monje's lust for power, and said to him:

"Look, Monje, if that's what's bothering you, I promise to get up early every morning, stand at attention in front of you, and say, 'Commander, give me my orders for the day,' and that way we can satisfy the CIA agent."

The meeting lasted several hours, but they never reached agreement. Monje asked Che to give him some time to think about what they had talked about, and Che agreed. Then Che invited Monje to go with him to the Main Camp to eat a typical Cuban dinner. After the meal, Monje asked Che to let him meet with the Bolivians in the guerrilla movement. One of them, Lorgio Vaca Marchetti, left that meeting and told Che that Monje ought to be shot, because he was threatening to expel them from the Bolivian Communist Party and not provide any kind of financial aid to their families if they didn't quit the guerrilla movement. There were a number of Bolivians in that meeting who opposed Monje, among them the Peredo Leigue brothers. The next day Monje left the Main Camp and we never saw him again. Che met with all the guerrillas and assured them that Monje's negative stance would not stand in the way of the armed struggle in Bolivia.

Occupation of the Bolivian army barracks in Samaipata[3]

Ricardo, Pacho, Coco, Ernesto (Freddy Maymura Hurtado), Julio (Mario Gutiérrez Ardays), and Chino (Juan Pablo Chang Navarro) took part in this action. On the outskirts of Samaipata they seized a truck to get to town and on arriving they saw that the barracks chief, a Bolivian army lieutenant, was sitting in the village park. They detained this officer and then Ricardo, Pacho, and Coco went with him to the barracks, where there were 10 soldiers. The other guerrillas went to buy food and medicine. When they reached the door of the barracks, which was closed, the lieutenant gave the password, followed by the counterpassword. As soon as the door was opened the three guerrillas rushed in and ordered everyone not to move. One soldier tried to open fire but Pacho got him with a rifle shot. They took all the weapons from the barracks and loaded all the soldiers onto the truck. Once outside Samaipata they were released, wearing only their underwear.

Although Che approved of the Samaipata action, he criticized those who took part for not having brought the necessary food or medicines, especially the medication he needed for his asthma, which he was suffering from very much in those days. Later we heard that the villagers had ridiculed the soldiers when they appeared in town wearing only their underpants.

During that time we heard over the radio that the leader of Bolivia's military regime had announced that Che was at the head of the guerrilla movement, and that the army was carrying out an offensive to wipe out the guerrillas. From then on the army's pursuit of the guerrilla unit got more intense.

On Che's death[4]

We had a feeling they were going to murder Che, like they had done with other captured guerrillas, because Che alive was a great threat to the imperialists and their allies. Had they put him on trial, the accused would have been transformed into the accuser, charging them with being enemies of the Latin America peoples. That same day we heard over a number of Bolivian radio stations that Che had died in battle. We all understood that the Bolivian army had killed him on orders from the Central Intelligence Agency (CIA), but no one imagined that the crime had been committed in La Higuera, because if we had known Che was there we wouldn't have hesitated to try to rescue him, even though it would have been a suicide mission.

---

1. The *Granma* was the yacht in which Fidel Castro, Guevara, and 80 other members of the July 26 Movement sailed to Cuba in November-December 1956 to initiate the revolutionary war against the Batista dictatorship.

2. Gen. Rodion Malinovsky was Soviet defense minister and commander of its land forces.

3. On July 6, 1967, a guerrilla squad captured and briefly occupied Samaipata, the capital of Florida province in Bolivia, causing an international sensation.

4. Guevara was wounded and captured Oct.8, 1967. After consulting Washington, the Bolivian government ordered his execution, which took place the following day at the La Higuera schoolhouse. Not knowing Guevara's fate, Urbano and the other five remaining guerrilla combatants had been within sight of the schoolhouse the night of October 8.

CHE IN THE CONGO: 'A RETURN TO OUR INTERNATIONALIST ROOTS'

by Ernesto Montero Acuña

The article below appeared in the Nov. 20, 1995, issue of *Trabajadores*, the weekly publication of the Central Organization of Cuban Workers, reporting on a conference that had just concluded. Translation and footnotes are by the *Militant*.

Fifty of the 370 Cuban internationalists who were part of the two columns headed by Che toward the end of 1965 in what are today the African republics of Zaire[1] and the Congo participated in an extensive and reflective look back at those events, held this past Saturday at the Central House of Cuba's Revolutionary Armed Forces [FAR]. At its conclusion, Division General Néstor López Cuba discussed the role of the FAR at present and said, "The mission today is the special period,[2] but without weakening defense." There were many key moments during this return to our internationalist roots.

TRICONTINENTAL

Che Guevara (right) with other Cuban fighters in the Congo, 1965.

A Latin-African people is how Fidel labeled us at the conclusion of the First Congress of the [Communist] Party at the Plaza of the Revolution in 1975. He was explaining the reasons for the Cuban internationalist mission in the People's Republic of Angola, which had just been proclaimed.[3]

Twenty years later one can better appreciate the relationship of that event to our heritage and also to the presence of Che's guerrilla unit in the Congo. Two columns of experienced Cuban combatants planted the seeds that later bore fruit on African soil.

Today we commemorate the 30th anniversary of that mission of solidarity, begun by the Heroic Guerrilla on April 24, 1965, in what was then Congo-Leopoldville, today the Republic of Zaire. On August 21 of that year, this mission was complemented by another column that aided the government of Congo-Brazzaville, today the Republic of the Congo. At the time, however, they were ready to reinforce Che's group.

Jorge Risquet Valdés, head of the political high command of that mission, recalled various circum-

Reprinted from *Militant* vol. 61, no. 45, Dec. 22, 1997.

stances of those events, together with some of the 50 participants in the seminar held last Saturday at the Central House of the FAR. The meeting commemorated the 30th anniversary of that act of solidarity with the struggle of Black Africa against colonial and neocolonial oppression, conceived by Che and the Cuban revolutionary leadership.

Brig. Gen. Harry Villegas, Hero of the Republic of Cuba and internationalist combatant in Column no. 1 in the Congo and in the Bolivian guerrilla movement, explained the adverse conditions they had to confront in an unfamiliar environment, with ethnic and cultural differences, a low level of development, and profound backwardness.

For Villegas, currently a member of the leadership of the Western Army, the mission that concluded Nov. 21, 1965, had proven to be effective in a brief period of time. It contributed to improving the medical care provided by the Cubans to the adult population and children, and was an important contribution to getting acquainted with one another.

In line with the seminar's reflective character, Jorge Risquet recalled that in Brazzaville, in early 1965, Che held "a meeting with the leadership of the MPLA, headed by Agostinho Neto," at which a commitment was made "at the request of the Angolan patriots" to aid their guerrilla movement in the fight against Portuguese colonialism, which led to deep and lasting internationalist cooperation.

Risquet, a member of the Central Committee of the Communist Party of Cuba, cited passages from the speech by General of the Army Raúl Castro, minister of the Revolutionary Armed Forces, at the event marking the 20th anniversary of both columns—the second of which concluded its mission in December 1966. In that speech Raúl highlighted the consequences of colonialism in Africa and America.

"Long before the aboriginal inhabitants in the Antilles were exterminated by the fire and lash of the conquistadores," Raúl said, "the Portuguese and Spaniards had already begun the shameful business of slave-trafficking, seizing ivory and rubber and especially the greatest wealth of all: African human beings."

He also pointed out how Che envisioned that in a "context of political ferment and increasing prominence by the African peoples . . . there was a need to offer solidarity to prevent the recolonization of Zaire and contribute to the armed struggle of the peoples of the Portuguese colonies. This was to be a starting point for the great and definitive battle: the liberation of the South African people from the abject yoke of apartheid and the independence of Namibia, also occupied by the white racists of Pretoria."

In his evaluation of that historic mission, the minister of the FAR hailed the intense combat activity of both columns, characterized by their member's daring and discipline. He also reviewed the numerous missions of Column no. 2, headed by Jorge Risquet and Brigadier General Rolando Kindelán Blez.

This column, in addition to constituting Che's reserve force to be incorporated when necessary and aiding the progressive government of the Congo, then threatened with aggression by the Kinshasa regime,[4] was also assigned to assist the Second Front of the MPLA in Cabinda, among other activities. The Cuban-Congolese-Angolan collaboration helped create the conditions for the struggle in Angola, in conquering and preserving that country's independence.

"In the difficult initial moments of Angola's second war of liberation," explained the second secretary of the party on the 20th anniversary of these columns, "Brazzaville served as a secure rear guard for one part of our troops. Its comradeship in arms with the MPLA—dating back to 1965—has become a factor of considerable importance in preserving the sovereignty and integrity of the People's Republic of Angola."

He then stated the following: "To spell things out, the course of history has confirmed . . . the validity of that mission, which already figures among the outstanding precedents of our internationalist course of action, which we will never renounce. It also helped clear open a path for the struggles of the peoples of Africa, to which the Revolutionary Armed Forces of Cuba has offered its determined support."

In his historical evaluation, Raúl stressed how those approximately 370 men have been "multiplied a thousand-fold in the noble endeavor of paying our debt of gratitude to humanity at the price of one's own life if necessary."[5] He stated that more than 120 carried out other internationalist missions, and several dozen of them participated in three, four, and even five missions. Of these combatants, more than 90 percent are members of the [Cuban Communist] party.

During the seminar, chaired by Division Generals Ulises Rosales del Toro, first deputy to the minister of the FAR and head of the general staff, and Néstor López Cuba, head of the Political Directorate of the FAR, a number of speakers made remarks reflecting the central importance of Cuba's collaboration in Africa.

In one very illustrative set of remarks, pediatrician Rodolfo Puentes Ferro explained the role of our doctors in Brazzaville, where infant mortality was very high. An incipient effort against poliomyelitis was begun; a hundred young people were selected to be trained in Cuba. In 1977, during his trip to the Congo, he was able to corroborate that 70 of them were doctors.

At the time of the 1960s mission, there was only one native-born doctor of medicine. Now there exists one for every 8,000 inhabitants, according to World Health Organization figures. In concluding his remarks, in which he referred to Doctors Rodrigo Alvarez Cambras, Luis Delgado, Manuel Jaca, and other doctors participating in the mission, he said that "the most important thing was the mark of our presence we left behind."

In contrast, the United States first ordered the assassination of Patrice Lumumba,[6] and later spent $45 million financing the white mercenaries in the Congo—located in the heart of Africa and possessing enormous mineral wealth. It equipped the repressive forces with arms and planes, and promoted massive crimes.

U.S. imperialism came to replace its Belgian and Portuguese peers. But it was unable to prevent the liberation of Angola, Namibia, Guinea-Bissau, or the defeat of apartheid in South Africa. All this was a result of those historic missions by the Cuban combatants in the Congo, headed by the Heroic Guerrilla.

It was a return to our Latin-African revolutionary roots.

---

1. Zaire was renamed Democratic Republic of the Congo following the overthrow of the regime of dictator Mobutu Sese Seko in May 1997.

2. "Special Period" is the term Cubans use to describe the economic crisis precipitated by the collapse in aid and trade from the Soviet Union at the opening of the 1990s.

3. Shortly before the Angolan government was to celebrate its formal independence from Portuguese colonial rule in November 1975, the country was invaded by troops from South Africa and Zaire. When the new regime led by the Popular Movement for the Liberation of Angola (MPLA) called for internationalist assistance, Cuban troops volunteered and turned back the invasion. Over the next 13 years, Cuban forces remained in Angola, helping defend the country's sovereignty against repeated attacks by the apartheid regime. A historic turning point in Africa came when Cuban volunteer troops, together with the Angolan army, defeated the South African forces at the battle of Cuito Cuanavale in 1988. This victory spurred an upsurge in South Africa that finally toppled the apartheid regime there. The last Cuban troops left Angola in 1991.

4. The dictatorship in Congo-Leopoldville.

5. More than 300,000 Cubans took part in the internationalist mission in Angola alone.

6. In January 1961 Patrice Lumumba, central leader of the Congo's independence movement, was murdered by imperialist-backed forces loyal to rightist figure Moise Tshombe.

'POMBO' SPEAKS ON CHE'S LEADERSHIP IN AFRICA

by Harry Villegas (Pombo)

From April 1965 until November of that year, Ernesto Che Guevara led a contingent of more than 100 Cuban volunteers in the Congo, aiding revolutionary forces fighting the pro-imperialist regime there. The article below on this internationalist effort appeared in a special issue of the magazine *Tricontinental*, published in Havana by the Organization of Solidarity of the Peoples of Africa, Asia, and Latin America. The author, Harry Villegas, who fought alongside Guevara in the Congo and later Bolivia, is today a brigadier general in Cuba's Revolutionary Armed Forces. The article was originally published under the title "With the Weapon of Moral Authority." Reprinted by permission. Translation, subheadings, and footnotes are by the *Militant*.

When I met him upon joining the Rebel Army in the Sierra Maestra mountains, Che was already an epic figure, the invincible commander, an example. Those were the qualities that help explain the great attraction he exercised on us, the young people there.

Those of us who fought and worked alongside him, first in Cuba, then in Africa and in Bolivia, always refer to a strict and demanding Che, for whom discipline was something fundamental, although it was a conscious discipline that the men internalized. This had great political significance for him, and he began by applying it to himself. It was to play an important role in the battles of the Congo.

TRICONTINENTAL

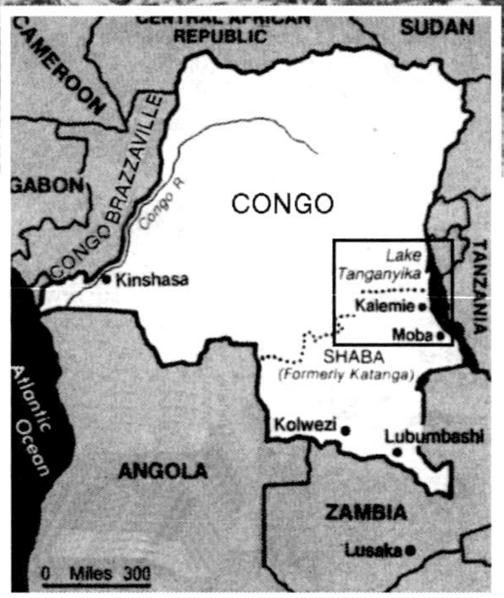

Cuban fighters in the Congo, 1965. **In the photo above,** Harry Villegas (Pombo), stands at right, with Che Guevara seated to the left of him. Box on map indicates approximate location of Che's column.

In 1965, on returning from his tour of Africa, Che was already convinced that he had done his part in Cuba.[1] He wanted to continue his mission in "other lands of the world," and he had decided to move on. At that time, his objective was not Africa but rather Latin America. As a way of realizing his desire to help other peoples, he agreed to the proposal to temporarily join the struggle in the Congo (Leopoldville), to head up a group of Cuban military personnel who would be supporting the struggle there. Among them, major re-

Reprinted from *Militant* vol. 61, no. 46, Dec. 29, 1997.

sponsibilities would be held by Víctor Dreke (Moya) and José María Martínez Tamayo (Mbili).

Fidel stuck to the agreement he had made with Che in Mexico, that he would allow Che to leave Cuba whenever the latter desired, regardless of the economic, political, or revolutionary circumstances.[2] But Fidel was also profoundly human, and he tried to repay Che, to some extent, for everything Che had done for Cuba. Fidel proposed to fulfill that moral commitment by providing Che with security, making sure that wherever Che went he would not be alone, and that he would have the support of the Cubans. That is also why many of us found ourselves there, voluntarily. In one way or another we were repaying our debt to humanity.

What was Africa like when we arrived?

It was difficult, practically impossible, for the group to fully comprehend that stage of social development. The customs were a tremendous shock to us. This was aggravated by the deficient cultural level that most of us possessed, although to tell the truth it wasn't easy for those who had a higher cultural level, either.

It was a mixture of primitive communism with feudalism, slavery, and matriarchy. Women provided for the sustenance of the family. They cultivated the land, carrying the children on their backs, while the men remained at home. We were very *machista* and weren't used to that; we didn't understand it and we resisted it.

There were also religious problems: the famous *dawa*, the fetish, with different forms and rituals in each zone, in each tribe. For example, when one said, "I am going to eat goat," they would warn us, "No, goats are sacred." We had to eat it and try to make them understand us, but it bothered them. They wound up concluding that we had a universal *dawa*, more powerful than theirs, which made us permanently immune. And therefore the one who had created that *dawa* for us, Fidel Castro, was the greatest *muganga* in the world.[3]

They could not go into combat without the protection of that fetish. They would form a long line to perform it on themselves, and during that time we would occupy defensive positions, turning ourselves into a shield to keep the enemy from arriving and to give them time to finish the ritual of the *dawa*.

Everything turned out to be very complicated. I, as head of the rear guard, was responsible for organizing the food. There were nearly 3,000 men, and all of them demanded their food be cooked individually. That would have put us in danger of being discovered from thousands of miles away due to the tremendous smoke plume it would have formed. Nevertheless, the best that could be arranged was to have them cook by platoons, 25 men, more or less.

Collaboration with Congolese fighters

So Che's first task, his permanent struggle, was to persuade us and make us understand this situation: that we were among an extremely backward people, who had been subjugated by the colonialists for more than four centuries.

When one saw the way he acted toward the Africans, one appreciated again Che's greatness, his extreme humility. He believed in the principle that collaboration involved a degree of subordination, although later on the experience in the Congo made him reconsider this tactic in the case of Bolivia, where he was more demanding with Mario Monje.[4]

His disposition to unconditional subordination explains why one could see him sitting in a hut waiting for months to be able to have a meeting with the main leaders of the National Liberation Army of the Congo (ELNC). This, after he had been an influential person in the building of socialism in Cuba, minister of industry, president of the National Bank and of the Central Planning Board. He was only able to have a brief discussion with Laurent-Desire Kabila, the second-in-command of the movement.

It was necessary that a native African assume the leadership of the movement in Kibamba. On arriving at this site, Che found a brave and capable man, Leonard Mitoudidi, who was the head of operations, but as chance would have it, Mitoudidi died after being there only a few days. Later Idelphonse Massengo was sent to take on responsibility as head of the general staff, and he found a degree of acceptance among the heads of the front, but not the amount required. He remained there the rest of the time, and continued the struggle after Che left. He died in combat, I am told.

I should point out that prior to our departure for the Congo, according to reports received in

Cuba, more than half the country had supposedly been liberated. But that wasn't the reality; the information was wrong. There were some inexact estimates, even in regard to geography. According to initial reports, the mountains came up almost to the shore of Lake Tanganyika, but that wasn't the case. The person who compiled the information had observed the coast at a distance from the lake.

The time came when Che determined that he could no longer wait for the leadership of the movement, and he decided to go to the battle front. Then a different phase began, one of marches, ambushes, attacks. It was in the assault on Front de Force, the most intense battle, that we lost some comrades.

The Cubans thought it wasn't a good idea for us to attack. Che thought so too, but he was flexible, and he accepted the proposal by the head of the front to launch an assault on Front de Force. The coordination of our actions broke down, and they were not carried out as planned. Basically, combat was supposed to begin with the impact of rockets we fired at the retaining wall of the dam at a hydroelectric station. That rocket strike was not carried out, but all the other forces continued their advance, penetrating the sectors of enemy fire.

The enemy troops, dug in at the bridge, had all the access routes well covered with mortars which they had aimed precisely at the roads beforehand. When combat began, it was very easy for them to launch a pinpoint artillery barrage with the mortars, because they had already adjusted their aim, and had practiced several times. They had prepared a good defense. This, together with our lack of coordination and the fact that many [Congolese] combatants retreated spontaneously, forced us to withdraw without having attained our objectives. This resulted in a hard blow for the morale of our people.

In any of the written accounts of Che's presence in Africa—among them for example, the one by General William Gálvez, *El sueño africano del Che*, [Che's African dream]—one can appreciate Che's very strong convictions, among which was his concept of the role that we Cubans were called on to play: that of educator, of social reformer. That's why he demanded that we always be an example, and he called on us to show great humility, capacity for sacrifice, and understanding of the particular circumstance, of the fact that all problems of attitude had a basis in social psychology, given the cultural difference between the two groups.

Che sought to maintain unity, morale

In the midst of a conjuncture in which a group of comrades wanted to return to Cuba, where there was a lack of internal cohesion among the various groups of the Congolese movement, and where there was distrust within the movement toward the Rwandans,[5] Che sought constantly to bind the different groups together, to maintain discipline and fighting morale, which were indispensable for guaranteeing the unity in struggle necessary to lead the war. This required him to be firm and demanding; he could not allow anything that might lead to chaos.

Faced with the obligation to solve these conflicts he was involved in, he appealed to persuasion, to convincing people, to his moral authority. He could do so because of the prestige he had gained in Cuba and because of that high degree of rigor, toward himself above all, which made him capable even of punishing himself if he committed an error.

One day we woke up to find a pile of rifles; the combatants had dropped them on the ground. Che called over a Congolese combatant and came to agreement with him on a reprimand, and that he should react by acknowledging that Che was right and picking up his weapon. Che began his talk in French, and the man forgot it all. Then Che told him, "Hey, my friend, hadn't we agreed that you'd pick up the rifle?" The Congolese picked up his weapon and all the others did the same. This gives you an idea of the psychological state that prevailed at that time.

We were already deep within Congolese territory when it was decided out of utter necessity that we should leave. Che analyzed all those internal conflicts. He wanted to go looking for Pierre Mulele, the head of one of the other three battle fronts, who was at the opposite end of the country. He would have had to travel almost to Brazzaville. Che's idea was to cross all the way through Zaire, in an invasion like the one the combatants of the Rebel Army had carried out from eastern Cuba to Las Villas[6] (in the central zone), only bigger—a huge march by nearly a thousand men, crossing a country of approximately three million square kilometers.

One must not forget that the presence of the Cuban column in the Congo (Leopoldville) depended to a certain extent on the policy laid out by the OAU [Organization of African Unity][7] at its meeting in Addis Ababa, of providing support only to national liberation movements, and not to internal struggles. By November 1965 there was an internal change, in which the dictator Moise Tshombe[8] (the one behind Patrice Lumumba's murder) was deposed. So the OAU reconsidered our presence there.

Che was authorized to decide whether we would leave, and in compliance with the mandate of the OAU he prepared for us to withdraw in the most organized fashion possible. But at the same time he strove to find someone in charge of the movement who would sign a document requesting the withdrawal of our forces. He wanted to make it very clear that we Cubans were not leaving the Congo voluntarily, but rather that we were compelled to do so by the conjuncture in the country.

No one appeared who would sign the document. We began to retreat toward the lake, under great pressure, evading the pursuit of airlifted troops. I remember Che's words about psychologically avoiding the idea of defeat, about how the loss of combativity eroded morale and became our most dangerous enemy. He told us about a Russian novel, in which a guerrilla detachment suffered those effects when it came up against the reality of a setback.

Our departure was quite complicated. The plan was to cross the lake before dawn in two small boats that Captain Lawton (Changa) had obtained. But that was impossible, and we had to leave by day. Bright sunlight caught us in the middle of that fresh-water sea, and the people were utterly exhausted.

We had installed a cannon on the boats, which we could not fire because the recoil itself would have destroyed the boat and wiped out all the men riding in it. Nevertheless, this stratagem served to convince the Congolese enemy, when they started to circle around us in two rapid Petit Vedette boats with Belgian crews, that we were capable of fighting. They avoided a confrontation, and let us pass. If they had decided to confront us, they could have cut us all to pieces with four shots. At the end of the day's journey, we got out.

Today I believe that the presence of Che in the Congo played a very important role from the psychological standpoint. It really contributed in a very positive way, and at the same time it had a powerful symbolism. The most important thing is the ideological message, the revolutionary message of fraternal cooperation, of sacrifice that he brought there, expressing the humanistic essence of the Cuban revolution and of Fidel.

---

1. Guevara made a three-month visit to Africa December 1964 to March 1965, advancing Cuba's relations with African governments and liberation movements. Among the countries he visited were Algeria, Mali, Congo-Brazzaville, Guinea, Ghana, Dahomey [Benin], Tanzania, and Egypt.

2. In 1987, Castro told an Italian journalist: "When [Che] joined us in Mexico . . . he did ask one thing: 'The only thing I want after the victory of the revolution is to go fight in Argentina . . . that no reasons of state will stand in the way.' And I promised him that."

3. A *muganga* was one who administered the *dawa,* which was supposed to protect a combatant from any kind of danger.

4. Mario Monje was the general secretary of the Communist Party of Bolivia. He sabotaged the revolutionary struggle led by Che in that country. Che rejected Monje's demand that Monje be the military commander of the guerrilla front.

5. A contingent of Rwandan volunteers was participating in the Congolese struggle.

6. A reference to the Rebel Army's westward march from the Sierra Maestra in eastern Cuba to the central province of Las Villas. It was conducted between August and October of 1958 by the columns led by Guevara and Camilo Cienfuegos. That effort helped seal the fate of the Batista dictatorship.

7. The OAU, which had originally called for world support to the struggle against the Congo regime led by Moise Tshombe and its Belgian and mercenary backers, changed its position when Tshombe was ousted October 13, 1965, and the new regime pledged to send the mercenaries home.

8. Patrice Lumumba was the leader of the Congolese struggle for independence from Belgium and the country's first prime minister in 1960. With the backing of the U.S. and Belgian governments, Moise Tshombe led a war against the Lumumba government that was aided by United Nations "peacekeeping" troops. Lumumba was murdered by Tshombe's forces in January 1961.

CHE GUEVARA, CUBA, AND THE ALGERIAN REVOLUTION

by Ahmed Ben Bella

The article below appeared in the October 1997 issue of the French publication *Le Monde diplomatique*, under the title, "On the 30th Anniversary of the Death of Che Guevara: Che as I knew him." Its author, Ahmed Ben Bella, was the central leader of the Algerian National Liberation Front, which led the struggle for independence from France. Ben Bella was the president of the revolutionary workers and farmers government that came to power following the victory over Paris in 1962. He was overthrown in a counterrevolutionary coup led by Col. Houari Boumediene in June 1965. The article is copyright ©1997 by *Le Monde Diplomatique*. Reprinted by permission. The translation, subheadings, and footnotes are by the *Militant*.

On October 9, 1967, in a little schoolroom in La Higuera, Bolivia, Ernesto "Che" Guevara was assassinated. He had been taken prisoner the day before. Thus ended the life of a revolutionary whom Jean-Paul Sartre called "the most complete human being of our era." It had led him from Argentina to Guatemala, from Cuba to the Congo, and finally to Bolivia, always inspired by an ardent hope of relieving the sufferings of the poor. President Ahmed Ben Bella met him many times in Algiers from 1962–65 when the city was a haven for all the anti-imperialists of the world.

For thirty years Che Guevara has been challenging our consciences. From beyond space and time, we hear Che's call, which demands that we answer: yes, only the revolution can sometimes transform man into a being of light. We saw this light illuminating his naked body lying somewhere in distant Ñancahuazú,[1] in the photographs that appeared in newspapers all over the world. The message of his final gaze continues to touch the depths of our soul.

Che was a courageous fighter, but a conscious one, with a body weakened by asthma. Sometimes, when I climbed with him to the Chréa heights overlooking the town of Blida, I saw him suffer an attack that turned him green in the face. Anyone who has read his Bolivian diary knows in what poor health he faced the terrible physical and mental ordeals with which his path was strewn.

It is impossible to speak of Che without speaking of Cuba and the special relations which united us, since his story and his life were so closely bound up with the country that became his second home before he turned to wherever the revolution called him.

I first met Ernesto "Che" Guevara in the autumn of 1962, on the eve of the international crisis around the missile affair and the United States blockade of Cuba.[2] Algeria had just achieved independence and formed its first government. As head of that government, I was due to attend the September 1962 session of the United Nations in New York at which the Algerian flag would be raised for the first time over the UN building, a ceremony marking the victory of our national liberation struggle and Algeria's entry into the concert of free nations.

Visits to Washington and Havana

The National Liberation Front's Political Bureau had decided that the trip to the United Nations should be followed by a visit to Cuba. More than just a

Reprinted from *Militant* Vol. 62, No. 4, Feb. 2, 1998.

visit, it was intended as an act of faith demonstrating our political commitment. Algeria wished to emphasize publicly its total solidarity with the Cuban revolution, especially at this difficult moment in its history.

I was invited to the White House on the morning of October 15, 1962 and had a frank and heated discussion about Cuba with the president, John Fitzgerald Kennedy. I asked him point blank: "Are you heading towards a confrontation with Cuba?" His reply left no doubt about his real intentions. "No," he said, "if there are no Soviet missiles. Yes, if there are." Kennedy tried hard to dissuade me from flying to Cuba direct from New York. He even suggested that the Cuban military aircraft that was to fly me to Havana might be attacked by Cuban opposition forces based in Miami. To these thinly veiled threats I retorted that I was a *fellaga* who could not be intimidated by *harkis*, whether Algerian or Cuban.[3]

Ahmed Ben Bella **(above, center)**, leader of the Algerian revolution, is welcomed to Havana in October 1962 by Cuban premier Fidel Castro **(above, left)**, Cuban president Osvaldo Dorticós (right), and an enthusiastic crowd. The day before Ben Bella got a much cooler reception from U.S. president John Kennedy in Washington **(right).**

We arrived in Cuba on October 16 amid indescribable scenes of popular enthusiasm. The program provided for political discussions at party headquarters in Havana immediately after our delegation arrived. But things worked out very differently. As soon as our luggage had been dropped off at the place where we were supposed to stay, we threw protocol overboard and began a heart-to-heart talk with Fidel, Che Guevara, Raúl Castro and the other leaders who were accompanying us.

We stayed and talked for hours and hours. I naturally conveyed to the Cuban leaders the impression I had received from my conversation with President Kennedy. At the end of an impassioned discussion, around tables which we had pushed together end-to-end, we realized that we had practically exhausted the questions on the agenda. There was no point in a further meeting at party headquarters, and by mutual consent we moved straight on to the program of visits prepared for us across the country.

This anecdote gives an idea of the total lack of formality that, from the very beginning, was the norm for the relations uniting the Cuban and Algerian revolutions and of my personal relations with Fidel Castro and Che Guevara.

Cuban troops aid Algerian revolution

The solidarity between us was spectacularly confirmed in October 1963, when the Tindouf campaign presented the first serious threat to the Algerian revolution.[4] Our young army, fresh from a war of liberation, had no air cover (since we didn't have a single plane) or armored transport. It was attacked by the Moroccan armed forces on the terrain that was most unfavorable to it, where it was unable to use the only tactics it knew and had tried and tested in the liberation struggle, namely guerrilla warfare.

The vast barren expanses of desert were far from the mountains of Aurès, Djurdjura, the Collo peninsula or Tlemcen, which had been its natural milieu and whose every resource and secret were familiar to it. Our enemies had decided that the momentum of Algerian revolution had to be broken before it grew too strong and carried everything in its wake.

The Egyptian president, Abdel Nasser, quickly provided us with the air cover we lacked, and Fidel Castro, Che Guevara, Raúl Castro and the other Cuban leaders sent us a battalion of 22 tanks and several hundred troops. They were deployed at Bedeau, south of Sidi Bel Abbès, where I inspected them, and were ready to enter into combat if the desert war continued.

The tanks were fitted with infra-red equipment that allowed them to be used at night. They had been delivered to Cuba by the Soviet Union on the express condition that they were not to be made available to third countries, even communist countries such as Bulgaria, in any circumstances. Despite these restrictions from Moscow, the Cubans defied all the taboos and sent their tanks to the assistance of the endangered Algerian revolution without a moment's hesitation.

The United States was clearly behind the Tindouf campaign. We knew that the helicopters transporting the Moroccan troops were piloted by Americans. The same considerations of international solidarity subsequently led the Cubans to intervene on the other side of the Atlantic, in Angola and elsewhere.

The circumstances surrounding the arrival of the tank battalion are worth recalling, since they illustrate better than any commentary the nature of our special relations with Cuba.

When I visited Cuba in 1962, Fidel Castro made a point of honoring his country's pledge to give us two billion old French francs worth of aid.[5] Because of Cuba's economic situation, the aid was to be provided in sugar rather than in currency. I objected, arguing that Cuba needed her sugar at that time more than we did, he would not take no for an answer.

About a year after our discussion, a ship flying the Cuban flag docked in the port of Oran. Along with the promised cargo of sugar, we were surprised to discover two dozen tanks and hundreds of Cuban soldiers sent to help us. A brief note from Raúl Castro, scribbled on a page torn out of an exercise book, announced this act of solidarity.

Obviously, we could not let the ship return empty. We filled it with Algerian products and, on the advice of Ambassador Jorge Serguera, added a few Berber horses. This was the start of a kind of barter between our two countries that was carried on in the name of solidarity and was entirely devoid of commercial considerations. Circumstances and constraints permitting, it was a distinctive feature of our relations.

Che's internationalist work in Africa

Che Guevara was acutely aware of the countless restrictions that hinder and weaken genuine revolutionary action—and indeed of the limits on any experiment, however revolutionary—as soon as it confronts directly or indirectly the implacable rules of the market and the huckster mentality. He denounced them publicly at the Afro-Asian Conference held in Algiers in February 1965.[6] Moreover, the painful terms on which the affair of the missiles installed in Cuba had been concluded, and the agreement between the Soviet Union and the United States, had left a bitter taste. I myself exchanged very tough words on the matter with the Soviet ambassador in Algiers. All of this, together with the situation prevailing in Africa, which seemed to have enormous revolutionary potential, led Che to the conclusion that Africa was imperialism's weak link. It was to Africa that he now decided to devote his efforts.

I tried to point out that perhaps this was not the best way to help advance the revolutionary maturity which was developing on our continent. An armed revolution can and must find foreign support, but it first has to create the internal resources on which to base its struggle. But Che Guevara insisted that his own commitment must be total and required his physical presence. He made several trips to Cabinda (Angola) and Congo-Brazzaville.

He refused my offer of a private plane to help disguise his movements, so I instructed Algerian ambassadors throughout the region to provide him with every assistance. Whenever he returned from sub-Saharan Africa, we spent long hours exchanging ideas. Each time he came back impressed by the fabulous cultural riches of the African continent but dissatisfied with his relations with the Marxist parties of the countries he had visited and irritated by their approach. His experience in Cabinda and subsequent contacts with the guerrilla struggle around Stanleyville were particularly disappointing.[7]

Meanwhile, parallel to Che's activity, we were pursuing another course of action to save the armed revolution in western Zaire. In agreement with Nyerere, Nasser, Modibo Keita, N'Krumah, Kenyata and Sekou Touré,[8] Algeria contributed by air-lifting arms via Egypt, while Uganda and Mali supplied military cadres. The rescue plan had been conceived at a meeting in Cairo convened on my initiative. We were beginning to implement it when we received a desperate cry for help from the leaders of the armed struggle. Despite our efforts, we were too late and the revolution was drowned in blood by the assassins of Patrice Lumumba.

During one of his visits to Algiers, Che Guevara informed me of a request from Fidel. Since Cuba was under close surveillance, there was no real chance of organizing the supply of arms and military cadres trained in Cuba to other Latin American countries. Could Algeria take over? Distance was no great handicap. On the contrary, it could work in favor of the secrecy vital for the success of such a large-scale operation.

I agreed, of course, without hesitation. We immediately began to establish organizational structures, placed under the direct control of Che Guevara, to host Latin American revolutionary movements. Soon representatives of all these movements moved to Algiers, where I met them many times together with Che.

Their combined headquarters were set up in the hills overlooking Algiers in a large villa surrounded by gardens which we had assigned to them because of its symbolic importance. The name of the Villa Susini has gone down in history. During the national liberation struggle it was used as an torture center where many men and women of the resistance met their death.

One day Che Guevara said to me, "Ahmed, we've just been struck a serious blow. A group of men trained at the Villa Susini have been arrested at the border between such and such countries (I can't remember the names) and I'm afraid they may talk under torture." He was very worried that the secret site of the preparations for armed action would become known and that our enemies would discover the true nature of the import-export companies we had set up in South America.

Che Guevara had left Algiers by the time of the military coup on June 19, 1965. He had warned me to be on my guard. His departure from Algeria, his death in Bolivia and my own disappearance for 15 years need to be studied in the historical context of the ebb that followed the period of victorious liberation struggles. After the assassination of Lumumba, it spelt the end of the progressive regimes of the third world, including those of N'Krumah, Modibo, Keita, Sukarno and Nasser, etc.[9]

The date October 9, 1967 is written in fire in our memory. For me, a solitary prisoner, it was a day of immeasurable sadness. The radio announced the death of my brother, and the enemies we had fought together celebrated their sinister victory. But as time passes, and the circumstances of the guerrilla struggle that ended that day in the Ñancahuazú fade from memory, Che, more than ever, is present in the thoughts of all those who struggle and hope. He is part of the fabric of their daily lives. Something of him remains attached to their heart and soul, buried like a treasure in the deepest, most secret, and richest part of their being, rekindling their courage and renewing their strength.

One day in May 1972, the opaque silence of my prison, jealously guarded by hundreds of soldiers, was broken by a tremendous din. I learnt that Fidel was visiting a model farm only a few hundred yards away, no doubt unaware of my presence in the secluded Moorish house on the hill whose roof he could glimpse above the treetops. It is certainly for the same reasons of discretion that this very house was, not so long ago, chosen as a torture center by the colonial army.

At this moment, the memories flooded back. A kaleidoscope of faces passed before my eyes like an old, faded newsreel. Never since we parted had Che Guevara been so vivid in my memory.

In reality, my wife and I have never forgotten him. A large photograph of Che was always pinned to the wall of our prison and his gaze witnessed our day-to-day life, our joys and our sorrows. But another smaller photo, cut out of a magazine, which I had stuck onto a piece of card and covered with plastic, accompanied us on all our wanderings and is the one that is closest to our hearts. It is now in my late parents' house in Maghnia, the village where I was born, where we deposited our most precious souvenirs before going into exile. It is the photograph of Ernesto "Che" Guevara stretched out on the ground, naked to the waist, blazing with light. So much light and so much hope.

---

1. The first guerrilla battle of Guevara's forces in Bolivia took place in the Ñancahuazú region, where the base camp for the combatants was located.

2. On Oct. 22, 1962, Kennedy initiated the "Cuban missile crisis," or October Crisis as it is known in Cuba. The U.S. president ordered a total blockade of Cuba, threatened an invasion of the island, and placed U.S. forces around the world on nuclear alert. Washington demanded the removal of Soviet nuclear missiles which had been installed in Cuba by mutual agreement of the two sovereign powers. Cuban workers and farmers responded by mobilizing massively in defense of the revolution. Faced with the determination of the Cuban people, and the knowledge that an assault on Cuba would result in massive U.S. casualties, Kennedy negotiated with Soviet premiere Nikita Khruschev, who decided to remove the missiles without consulting the Cuban government.

3. *Fellaga*, the Arabic term for "outlaw" or "bandit", was used by pro-independence fighters in Algeria to identify themselves defiantly in face of the French colonial rulers, which tried to slander them with that label. *Harkis* were counterrevolutionary auxiliary troops organized by the French colonial army in North Africa.

4. In 1963 Moroccan forces, backed by Washington, invaded Algeria, which had won its independence from France the previous year after an eight-year revolutionary war. At Algeria's request, the Cuban government sent a column of troops under the command of Efigenio Ameijeiras, a veteran of the Cuban revolutionary war, to help stop the attack. The mere presence of Cuban troops forced the Moroccan government to back down and withdraw its forces.

5. Approximately $3.3 million at current exchange rates.

6. This speech appears in *Che Guevara Speaks*, published by Pathfinder Press.

7. Stanleyville was the former name of Kisangani, in the Democratic Republic of Congo (formerly Zaire). Between April and December 1965, Guevara led a contingent of more than 100 Cuban volunteers assisting revolutionary forces that were fighting the regime in Congo, which was backed by Belgian, South African, and other imperialist forces. In January 1961 Patrice Lumumba, the leader of the fight for independence from Belgium and first prime minister of the Congo, had been murdered by proimperialist forces backed by Washington, after being disarmed by a U.S.-led United Nations "peacekeeping" intervention.

8. The presidents of Tanganyika (now Tanzania), Egypt, Mali, Ghana, Kenya, and Guinea respectively.

9. Indonesian president Sukarno was overthrown after a 1965 military coup.

RELATED READING

Episodes of the Cuban Revolutionary War, 1956–58

ERNESTO CHE GUEVARA

A firsthand account of political events and military campaigns that culminated in the January 1959 popular insurrection that overthrew the US-backed dictatorship in Cuba. With clarity and humor, Guevara describes his own political education. He explains how the struggle transformed the men and women of the Rebel Army and July 26 Movement, opening the first socialist revolution in the Americas. $23

Che Guevara Speaks

In twenty speeches, interviews, and letters, Guevara dissects the workings of the imperialist system with scientific clarity, truthfulness, and biting humor. Cuba has shown by its example, he says, that "a people can liberate themselves and keep themselves free." $15. Also in Farsi.

The Bolivian Diary of Ernesto Che Guevara

Guevara's day-by-day chronicle of the 1966–67 guerrilla campaign in Bolivia, an effort to forge a continent-wide revolutionary movement of workers and peasants and extend the socialist revolution to South America. $23. Also in Spanish.

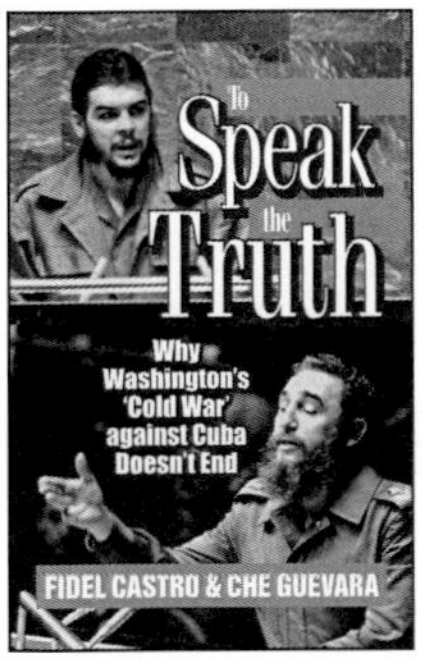

To Speak the Truth

Why Washington's 'Cold War' against Cuba Doesn't End

FIDEL CASTRO, CHE GUEVARA

In historic speeches before the United Nations and UN bodies, Guevara and Castro address the peoples of the world, explaining why the US government so fears the example set by the socialist revolution in Cuba and why Washington's efforts to destroy it will fail. $15

New Edition!

Che Guevara on Economics and Politics in the Transition to Socialism

CARLOS TABLADA

It's essential for working people to win state power, said Ernesto Che Guevara. "Then there's the second stage, maybe more difficult than the first"—the transition from dog-eat-dog capitalism to socialism. That includes moving from work as a condition for survival, to voluntary social labor through which we express our common humanity. Includes Fidel Castro's 1987 speech "Che's Ideas Are Absolutely Relevant Today." New edition with substantially expanded selections from Guevara's writings. $17. Also in Spanish, coming in French.

Women in Cuba: The Making of a Revolution within the Revolution

VILMA ESPÍN
ASELA DE LOS SANTOS
YOLANDA FERRER

The integration of women in the ranks and leadership of the Cuban Revolution was intertwined with the proletarian course of the leadership of the revolution from the start. This is the story of that revolution and how it transformed the women and men who made it. $17. Also in Spanish, Farsi, Greek.

Pombo: A Man of Che's *guerrilla*

With Che Guevara in Bolivia, 1966–68

HARRY VILLEGAS ("POMBO")

A diary and account of the guerrilla campaign in Bolivia led by Ernesto Che Guevara. The author, a member of Che's general staff there and later a brigadier general in Cuba's Revolutionary Armed Forces, commanded five surviving guerrillas who eluded encirclement by the Bolivian army and US intelligence forces for more than four months. $20

THE WORKING CLASS AND THE FIGHT AGAINST JEW-HATRED

New!

The Fight Against Jew-Hatred and Pogroms in the Imperialist Epoch

Stakes for the International Working Class

V.I. LENIN, LEON TROTSKY
FARRELL DOBBS
JAMES P. CANNON
JACK BARNES
DAVE PRINCE

Jew-hatred and pogroms—like Hamas carried out on October 7, 2023—are now part of the permanent social convulsions and wars of the imperialist epoch. That's why fighting Jew-hatred is of decisive importance to the working class and oppressed nations of the entire world. The authors answer the all-important question: *What is to be done to end it*—for all time. $10. Also in Spanish, soon in French.

The Low Point of Labor Resistance Is Behind Us

The Socialist Workers Party Looks Forward

JACK BARNES
MARY-ALICE WATERS
STEVE CLARK

The global order imposed by Washington after its victory in World War II is shattering. A long retreat by the working class and unions has come to an end. The bosses and their government are stepping up attacks on our wages, conditions, and constitutional rights. This book highlights opportunities for building a mass proletarian party able to lead the struggle to end capitalist rule, opening a socialist future for humanity. $10. Also in Spanish and French.

The Founding of the Socialist Workers Party

Minutes and Resolutions, 1938–39

JAMES P. CANNON

$23

Capitalism's World Disorder

Working-Class Politics at the Millennium

JACK BARNES

The social devastation and financial panic, coarsening of politics, cop brutality, and imperialist aggression—all are products not of something gone wrong with capitalism but of its lawful workings. Yet the future can be changed by the united struggle of workers and farmers increasingly conscious of their capacity to wage revolutionary struggles for state power and to transform the world. $20. Also in Spanish and French.

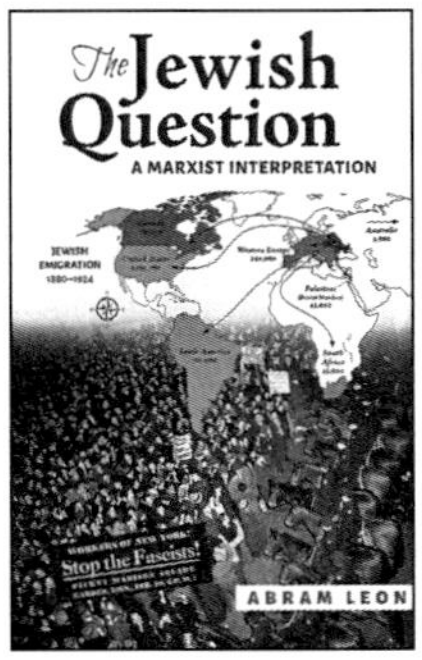

The Jewish Question

A Marxist Interpretation

ABRAM LEON

The battle against reactionary forces aiming to exterminate the Jews remains central to world politics, as shown by the genocidal October 2023 pogrom in Israel. Why is Jew-hatred still raising its ugly head? What are its class roots? Why, as Abram Leon explains, is there no solution "independent of the world proletarian revolution"? Revised translation, new introduction, and 40 pages of illustrations and maps. $17. Also in Spanish and French.

Imperialism's March toward Fascism and War

JACK BARNES

"There will be new Hitlers, new Mussolinis. That is inevitable. What is not inevitable is that they will triumph. The working-class vanguard will organize our class to fight back against the devastating toll we are made to pay for the capitalist crisis. The future of humanity will be decided in the contest between these contending class forces." In *New International* no. 10. $14. Also in Spanish, French, Farsi, Greek.

CAPITALIST CRISIS AND THE FIGHT FOR WORKERS POWER

Are They Rich Because They're Smart?

Class, Privilege, and Learning under Capitalism

JACK BARNES

In battles forced on us by the capitalists, workers will begin to transform our attitudes toward life, work, and each other. We'll discover our worth, denied by the rulers and upper middle classes who insist they're rich because they're smart. We'll learn in struggle what we're capable of becoming. $10. Also in Spanish, French, Farsi, Arabic, Greek.

The Clintons' Anti-Working-Class Record

Why Washington Fears Working People

JACK BARNES

What working people need to know about the profit-driven course of Democrats and Republicans alike over the last three decades. And the political awakening of workers seeking to understand and resist the capitalist rulers' assaults. $10. Also in Spanish, French, Farsi, Greek.

Cuba and the Coming American Revolution

JACK BARNES

This is a book about the example set by the Cuban people that socialist revolution is not only necessary—it can be made. A book about the struggles of workers and other exploited producers in the imperialist heartland, and the youth attracted to them. About the class struggle in the US, where the revolutionary capacities of working people are as utterly discounted by the ruling powers as were those of the Cuban toilers. And just as wrongly. $10. Also in Spanish, French, Farsi.

Labor, Nature, and the Evolution of Humanity

The Long View of History

FREDERICK ENGELS
KARL MARX
GEORGE NOVACK
MARY-ALICE WATERS

Without understanding that social labor, transforming nature, has driven humanity's evolution for millions of years, working people are unable to see beyond the capitalist epoch of class exploitation that warps all human relations, ideas, and values. Only the revolutionary conquest of state power by the working class can open the door to a world free of capitalist exploitation, degradation of nature, subjugation of women, racism, and war. A world built on human solidarity. A socialist world. $12. Also in Spanish and French.

The Communist Manifesto

KARL MARX AND FREDERICK ENGELS

Communism, say the founding leaders of the revolutionary workers movement, is not a set of ideas or preconceived "principles" but workers' line of march to power, springing from a "movement going on under our very eyes." $5. Also in Spanish, French, Farsi, Arabic.

Teamster Rebellion

FARRELL DOBBS

The 1934 strikes that won union recognition for truckers and warehouse workers in Minneapolis and helped pave the way for the working-class social movement that built the industrial unions. The first of four volumes by a central leader of these battles. $16. Also in Spanish, French, Farsi, Greek.

WORKING-CLASS LEADERSHIP AND THE SOCIALIST REVOLUTION

Thomas Sankara Speaks

The Burkina Faso Revolution, 1983–87

Under Sankara's guidance, Burkina Faso's revolutionary government led peasants, workers, women, and youth to expand literacy; to sink wells, plant trees, erect housing; to combat women's oppression; to carry out land reform; to join others worldwide to free themselves from the imperialist yoke. $20. Also in French.

Lenin's Final Fight

Speeches and Writings, 1922–23

V.I. LENIN

In 1922 and 1923, V.I. Lenin, central leader of the world's first socialist revolution, waged what was to be his last political battle—one that was lost after his death. At stake was whether that revolution, and the international communist movement it led, would remain on the revolutionary proletarian course that brought workers and peasants to power in October 1917. $17. Also in Spanish, Farsi, Greek.

Malcolm X Speaks

"Being here in America doesn't make you an American. No, I'm not an American. I'm one of the 22 million Black people who are the victims of Americanism. One of the 22 million Black people who are the victims of democracy, nothing but disguised hypocrisy." $15. Also in Spanish.

Socialism on Trial

Testimony at Minneapolis Sedition Trial

JAMES P. CANNON

The revolutionary program of the working class, presented in response to frame-up charges of "seditious conspiracy" in 1941, on the eve of US entry into World War II. The defendants were leaders of the Minneapolis labor movement and the Socialist Workers Party. $15. Also in Spanish, French, Farsi.

Rosa Luxemburg Speaks

EDITED BY MARY-ALICE WATERS

Rosa Luxemburg's place of honor among the great revolutionary Marxist leaders of the twentieth century has often been denied her. Here she speaks for herself, with clarity and wit, taking on political battles that continue to divide revolutionaries from reformists in the workers movement even a century after her murder in Berlin in 1919 by counterrevolutionary militias. $25

Puerto Rico: Independence Is a Necessity

RAFAEL CANCEL MIRANDA

One of the five Puerto Rican Nationalists imprisoned by Washington for more than 25 years and released in 1979 speaks out on the brutal reality of US colonial domination, the example of Cuba's socialist revolution, and the ongoing struggle for independence. $5. Also in Spanish and Farsi.

Eugene V. Debs Speaks

Speeches by the pioneer US socialist agitator and labor leader, jailed for opposing Washington's imperialist aims in World War I. Debs speaks out on capitalism and socialism, anti-immigrant chauvinism, how anti-Black racism weakens the labor movement, Rockefeller's massacre of striking miners at Ludlow, Colorado, and more. $17